BEDFORD

St Luke's

A BIT OF CHURCH HISTORY

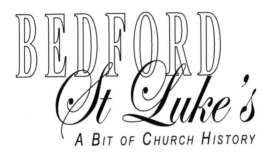

BEDFORD
St Luke's
A BIT OF CHURCH HISTORY

DAVID BUNNEY

ATHENA PRESS
LONDON

ISBN 978 1 84748 694 3

First published 2010 by
ATHENA PRESS
Queen's House, 2 Holly Road
Twickenham TW1 4EG
United Kingdom

Printed for Athena Press

Thanks are expressed to the following
for their cooperation in supplying information:
Gwen Gribble, Marion Swift, Cathie Stewart and Nancy Barr.

Contents

Foreword

The adventure began when the then-Moderator of the Thames North Synod of the United Reformed Church, the Rev. Roberta Rominger, chose to sit beside the writer on a coach outing during a visit to the newly formed United Protestant Church of the Netherlands in May 2004. The conversation centred on music, the moderator being an accomplished cellist and the writer a trained singer. A fortnight or so later, the moderator of the Eastern Synod, the Rev. Elisabeth Caswell, visited the writer in his Suffolk pastorate and gave him the pastoral profile of St Luke's United Church, Bedford; at the time the pastorate was vacant. Thus began the series of meetings and consultations, which resulted in an invitation to Bedford. The service of induction took place on the eve of Advent Sunday in November 2004.

The profile envisaged the setting up of a three-way Local Ecumenical Partnership (LEP), which would embrace the Moravian, United Reformed and Anglican traditions and that would have made a significant statement to the town-centre churches in Bedford. St Luke's United Church had grown from four different, if overlapping, roots into a significant and respected force for mission and witness. Sadly, its great potential was not to flourish. It was soon realised that the keen interest which had built up under the previous minister, the Rev. David Tatem (who had moved on to the Church of Christ the Cornerstone in Milton Keynes), and the Rector of St Peter's, the Rev. Guy Buckler (who now chose to move on for family reasons to Bushey), had diminished.

The state of the buildings, the finances and the current level of support pointed to huge difficulties in the longer term. The decision to move towards closure, when it was finally taken, resulted in an easing of the tensions that were beginning to show in the St Luke's community, and the necessary steps were taken to enable this to be accomplished. The final acts of worship were held on Sunday, 5 October 2008, after which the site and the buildings were sold. Thus a long and distinguished history of Christian witness and fellowship came to an end, a history that had seen significant contributions to religious and civic life in so many different ways.

This work is an attempt to chronicle and acknowledge those contributions, as a way of expressing thanks to all who contributed to the life of St Luke's and made its achievements possible.

The help of many people is acknowledged with grateful thanks, especially that of Marion Swift and Gwen Gribble, whose contributions and constructive criticisms have been helpful and much appreciated, as has been the encouragement of Richard Wildman.

David R Bunney

The front exterior of St Luke's flanked by the two red-brick buildings which housed the former Sisters' House and the Minister's House photo by Marion Swift.

Introduction

Anyone coming to worship at St Luke's United Church, Bedford, during the early summer of 2008 would have felt an immense sadness. To reach the church door they had to pass a simple sign with the words 'For Sale'. After 263 years of Christian service on the site, the members of the present congregation had had to acknowledge that their resources were no longer sufficient to enable them to continue. The planned closure would bring to an end a significant part of Bedford's long and distinguished place in the history of reasoned dissent.

The writer grew up in a Bedfordshire village and went to school in the town. Although his family was active in Free Church circles in the post-war years, sharing in such events as the National Sunday School Union's annual Scripture Examination and enjoying occasional visits by prominent figures in Free Church life such as Lord Soper and Sandy Macpherson, St Luke's did not feature among them; it appeared to be, as it was perceived for much of its time, to one side of the life of the town's churches and community. It could be said that Moravianism has always occupied such a position, seeking not to establish itself as a separate entity so much as to reinforce the service to the Gospel of Jesus Christ, wherever that might be expressed.

As the date of closure drew near, a number of people came through the church door to look in out of curiosity, saying, 'I've never been in here before.' Perhaps its decline was due to the fact that recently it had 'only' been used for Christian worship! Society today seems unable to cope with anything serious.

The purpose of this present historical survey is to draw attention to the enormous wealth of Christian experience that has been enacted in and through St Luke's United Church and, despite its apparent reticence, to highlight something of its enormous legacy to the town and community of Bedford and the affection in which it was held.

11

The church in its later years was an amalgam of four parts of the old Protestant dissenting tradition: four elements that remind one, of course, of the four arms of the cross of Christ. This was reflected in four evening talks held during the last month of the church's work (September 2008), given by distinguished representatives of the four denominational traditions. Following the generic title 'What it means to be…', the Moravian heritage was outlined by the Rt Rev. John McOwat, Bishop of the Unity in the British Province; the Presbyterian heritage by Professor the Rev. Dr Alan Sell, formerly theological secretary of the World Alliance of Reformed Churches in Geneva; the Congregational heritage by Professor the Rev. Dr Stephen Orchard who, before serving as moderator of the General Assembly of the United Reformed Church in 2007–08, had been Principal of Westminster College, Cambridge; and the Reformed heritage was explored by the Rev. Dr Janet Tollington, director of Old Testament Studies at Westminster College since 1994. Each of these was well presented and well supported. Further reference to this will follow.

Bedford St Luke's was originally a Moravian foundation in 1745, known as the Bedford Congregation. The name of St Peter's Moravian Church was adopted in 1895 to distinguish it from the newly founded Queen's Park Moravian Church. Members of Bedford's embryonic Presbyterian Church asked to share the premises for worship in 1952. This grew into a formal relationship, which was recognised in the formation of St Luke's Church in 1960.

New housing estates now known as Putnoe and Brickhill were spreading to the north and east of the town, and other Free Churches moved out from the town centre to serve them, including St Paul's Methodist from Harpur Street (where the town library now stands) to Priory in Newnham Avenue, Bromham Road Methodist to Putnoe Heights, and Mill Street Baptist to Brickhill Drive. In 1969 the last minister left Howard Congregational Church, also in Mill Street, and was not replaced. That church had been founded in 1775, with John Howard as principal benefactor; it was given his name in 1849. With the imminent formation of the United Reformed Church, its members also sought to join St Luke's in 1970; the church became a constituent member of the new United Reformed Church in 1972, reflecting the ecumenical position the Moravian Church had shown from the outset.

In 1984, a new structure was agreed and St Luke's United Church was formally constituted. Its closure would leave the Bunyan Meeting, which enjoys observer status with the United Reformed Church, as the sole representative of this reformed dissenting tradition in the town. When St Luke's closed, some of the members moved to Bunyan, further cementing the relationship that already existed. Others moved to the parish church of St Peter de Merton with St Cuthbert, where the writer shared in the ministry team until Easter, 2009.

The Christian presence in Bedford has been considerably diminished by the loss of this vibrant and deeply spiritual congregation, which it has been an enormous privilege to serve. It is hoped that this brief reflection of its life and history will both engage and inform, and serve as a fitting testimony to what the Moravian presence in the town has meant, what it later facilitated and what it has achieved over the years. The simple faith on which it was all based is summed up in the ancient Moravian principle, variously attributed but commonly accepted:

> In things essential, unity;
> In non-essentials, liberty;
> In all things, charity.

The Background in Bedford

The origins of the town of Bedford are Anglo-Saxon, its name coming from the fact that it was a ford, or crossing place, of the River Ouse; Beda was a leader of the community in the fifth century. Bedford's Christian history goes back to the seventh century, when what was to develop into St Paul's Church was a so-called minster church, a focus for service to the surrounding area. When the Danes invaded eastern Britain in the ninth century, the river was navigable as far as the town, which stood on a prominent ridge. The river marked the boundary between Danish and English territory: King Alfred ruled to the south and west, the Danish King Guthrum to the north and east.

After the Norman Conquest, Bedford became the county town of the shire, the baronetcy having been awarded to the Beauchamp family. The castle, of which only the mound remains, dominated the northern bank of the river. It saw action during the reign of King Stephen in 1138, and the town was granted its royal charter by Henry II in 1166, confirming its status as a market town. A bridge has spanned the river at its heart since at least 1200. The castle was destroyed in 1224 by followers of Henry III. Some of its stone was used to repair the bridge, on which at one time stood a chapel, similar to the one in neighbouring St Ives. It was used at one time as the lock-up. Prisons were to feature significantly in Bedford's later history.

The town remained more or less within its medieval limits until the nineteenth century and the expansion of manufacturing. This was primarily of agricultural implements to serve the farming community of the countryside. There had been a number of religious houses in or near the town, which were all closed down at the time of the Reformation; Bedford became a Protestant town, with several parishes established which still survive. The Roman Catholic Church did not reappear in the town until the 1860s. St Paul's remains the main church, its building having been substantially altered several times. In his book *England's Thousand Best Churches*[1] Simon Jenkins refers to it as 'a shrine to an old English borough at prayer'.

One of the main links with earlier times still in existence is the parish church of St Peter de Merton, with its Saxon chancel and tower and a Norman doorway (in the south porch); this actually came from the church of St Peter de Dunstable south of the river, and was moved in Tudor times. The organ console in the choir sits beneath a Saxon arch. There has been a church on this site for more than a thousand years; the present building was extensively restored during the nineteenth century. It was to be the new home of some of the congregation of St Luke's after its closure.

Sir William Harpur was born in Bedford in 1496. As a successful merchant, he rose to be Lord Mayor of London, and bought land in Holborn. The profits from this estate enabled him to endow two schools for boys: Bedford School in 1552, followed by what became known as Bedford Modern School (now co-educational) in 1566. Further expansion followed in the latter part of the nineteenth century, with Bedford High School and what was to become the Dame Alice Harpur School making provision for girls. Bedford School's site adjoined that of St Luke's and was also to feature after closure.

In Georgian times, Bedford became quite an elegant place, with the Swan Inn beside the river and the old Shire Hall gracing the area around the new town bridge. The eighteenth century was a quiet period in the history of the churches. After the strictures of the Puritan period, music was once again becoming a feature, and in 1715 St Paul's installed the organ which would later find a new home at St Luke's. Shortly after the dawn of the Moravian presence in the town, John Wesley preached the Assize Sermon in St Paul's in 1758.

St Paul's Church itself was rebuilt and extended in 1868 when the tower and spire were reconfigured, then again in 1884 with the addition of a north aisle. Methodism began to make an impression on the country as a whole, and in Bedford there was sufficient support to warrant establishing a Bedfordshire circuit. The Bedfordshire Union of Christians was set up in 1797, an

---

[1] Simon Jenkins, *England's Thousand Best Churches*, London, Penguin, 1999

early attempt at ecumenical cooperation. Soon after this, in 1804, what was to grow into St Paul's Methodist Church in Harpur Street was opened. It too was extended several times in the nineteenth century until it had a thousand seats. Bedford's Anglican churches had been in the huge diocese of Lincoln, but came into that of Ely in 1837 in a widespread revision of boundaries. Further revision saw the creation of the Diocese of St Albans in 1877, to which they still belong.

Two statues commemorate Bedford's two most famous sons: the figure of John Bunyan was created by Sir Edgar Boehm, a distinguished Victorian sculptor, and erected on St Peter's Green in 1874, the gift of the Ninth Duke of Bedford. It was cast from metal taken from cannons and bells captured in the Chinese War. The pensive figure of John Howard stands on St Paul's Square and was the creation of Alfred Gilbert in 1890, marking the centenary of his death. When recent restoration work was undertaken in 2005, it was reported that the statue was not actually attached to its plinth!

John Bunyan was born near the village of Elstow in 1628. His father was a tinker, a trade he was later to take up himself. The museum at the Bunyan Meeting includes his anvil, dated 1647. He was involved in the Civil War on the Parliamentary side, based in Newport Pagnell and his experience of army life influenced him greatly. He married a poor girl from Elstow and plied his trade in the town and in the local villages, but a sermon on the evils of breaking the Sabbath played on his mind and his life changed.

In 1653, he joined the new independent fellowship which met at St John's Church, and was deeply influenced by John Gifford, a convert who had become the incumbent. This experience led to the later creation of the character of the Interpreter in *The Pilgrim's Progress*. Bunyan soon began to preach, which was of course illegal – only those authorised by the established Church were allowed to do so. He persisted, and was arrested, then imprisoned until such time as he should agree to conform. He spent twelve years in the prison, which in those days stood at the present junction of Silver Street and High Street – a plaque in the pavement marks the site. During this time he continued to preach to his fellow prisoners, and to make lace, which helped to support his family. Later legislation allowed a degree of religious freedom, and he was released in 1672. Freedom was brief, and further imprisonment followed; at the time he lived in a cottage in St Cuthbert's Street, and his second arrest was for not taking the Anglican sacrament in his parish church.

During this incarceration he wrote his greatest work, *The Pilgrim's Progress*, which was published in 1678. Bunyan continued to preach and to serve in various ways. His eventual death was brought about by getting very wet while travelling back to London from Reading after a mission to reconcile a father and son. He died in 1688 and was buried in Bunhill Fields in London's City Road.

John Howard was born in 1726 in London, where he went to school and was apprenticed to a grocer. His father died when John was sixteen, leaving him with a fortune that he first used to travel in Italy and France, where he was briefly imprisoned in Brest. He became ill and returned to London. He married the older lady who cared for him, but she died soon afterwards. Howard moved to Cardington, where he had inherited land, and where he worked for the community, rebuilding cottages and providing education for the children. He married again, but his second wife also died.

He became High Sheriff of Bedfordshire in 1773, an unlikely appointment at that time for a Dissenter. The post included oversight of the county gaol. He was appalled at the conditions he found there, not least the degree of corruption among the guards, and, drawing on his own experience of imprisonment, set out to reform conditions for all prisoners. He published *The State of the Prisons* in 1777. He travelled extensively in this country and abroad and was instrumental in initiating legislation to ensure humane treatment for prisoners everywhere. Like Bunyan, he died after being caught in wet weather; Howard was visiting the Ukraine, where he is buried. The centenary of his death was marked by the erection of the statue, but it is sad to record that there was very little acknowledgement of the bicentenary in 1990.

This sets something of the background to the witness that was centred on St Luke's during the 263 years of its existence. It may not have achieved international or even national fame, but in its own small way it furthered the work of Christian service to the community that had marked so much of Bedford's past.

The Moravian Heritage

The Moravian Church was originally established in Bohemia and Moravia, well before the great Protestant Reformation. The date from which its history is measured today is 1457, preceding the movement in Germany by some sixty years. It arose principally out of the work and teaching of Jan Hus (c.1372–1415) who was dean of the Faculty of Philosophy at the University of Prague. This was the time of the sale of indulgences to finance the work of rebuilding the Basilica of St Peter in Rome, which in the early fifteenth century was in a very poor state of repair.

In 1412 representatives of the Pope arrived in the city of Prague to set up stalls in all its churches to facilitate such sales. Hus, then preacher at the Bethlehem Chapel, refused to allow this. The early stirrings of dissent were fuelled by the chapel statutes that demanded preaching be in the local language. In all this he was greatly influenced by the work of John Wycliffe, the English Reformer whose work had been centred mainly in Oxford. Wycliffe wanted to stress the importance of each individual person in the sight of God. Hus was summoned to defend himself at the Synod of Constance, but all to no avail. He was condemned, unfrocked and burned at the stake as a heretic. This was in Constance on 6 July 1415, the date of his birthday.

In the fifteenth century, the kingdom of Bohemia (now part of the Czech Republic) was being torn apart by civil and religious unrest. So, too, was the Roman Catholic Church, with rival popes in Rome and Avignon. In protest against what they saw as moral corruption and political activity within the Roman Church, a group of faithful people in 1457 withdrew to a remote village called Kunwald. There they established a community that tried to live in brotherly fellowship according to the principles set out in the Sermon on the Mount. They adopted the name of Jednota Bratrska (Unity of Brethren), which in Latin gave the name Unitas Fratrum; this is still the official name for the Moravian Church.

This community made progress, and soon began to look for signs that they were on the right road. Help was sought from a Waldensian bishop, Stephen. His willingness to help was seen as confirmation of their intentions. One priest who had joined them was consecrated bishop, who in turn ordained others. Thus they established their own episcopal orders, marking the completion of their separation from the Church of Rome. With this action they became one of the earliest independent Protestant churches. A new hymn was written in celebration of their new status, still in use among Moravians today. It begins with the words, 'Come, let us all with gladness raise a joyous hymn of thanks and praise.'[2]

The translation used is by Bishop Evelyn Hasse who served the Bedford Church from 1894 to 1906. The Brethren produced the first Protestant hymn book in the vernacular in 1501. Later in the century their scholars printed a translation of the Bible (known as the Kralitz Bible) that set a new standard for the Czech language and literature. Education was always an important part of the work of the growing Church, and each part established its own school. Two Moravian schools still function in this country, at Fulneck in Pudsey (between Leeds and Bradford) and at Ockbrook, near Derby.

Life was not easy for the new community. Despite increasing opposition, they had grown to a quarter of a million followers by the early sixteenth century. This did not escape the notice of the Vatican, and an edict was issued demanding that they either retracted and returned to the Catholic faith, or left the country. This was the time of the Habsburg supremacy of central Europe, part of the Holy Roman Empire dominated by the Catholic Church. In 1628, many of the Brethren left for Poland and other parts of Europe, where enclaves of German people had established themselves. Others struggled on, drawing encouragement from contacts with the reformers of Germany, France and Switzerland. Efforts to achieve a wider unity were not successful, and the Church suffered greatly during the Thirty Years War (1618–1648), especially in Bohemia. For a time it was thought they had been wiped out, but a small company remained, meeting

---

[2] 'Come let us all with gladness raise' quoted from the Moravian Hymn Book 1960 edition

secretly in the villages of Moravia. From such inauspicious settings came a leader of considerable distinction in Jan Arnose Komensky, better known in the English-speaking world as John Amos Comenius (1592–1670).

Comenius was the headmaster of the school in Fulnek in Moravia, where he developed some very advanced ideas about education – it was therefore appropriate that the premises of St Luke's would eventually come into school ownership. He longed for the unity of all Christians, and saw education as the means to achieving this end. The key lay not so much in learning as in following Christian principles. He is regarded as the father of modern education, and his advice was sought in many European countries, including England. When he left Bohemia it was his prayer that a 'hidden seed … might lie unseen, even forgotten, and at last take root and spring up to life'. He left material for those worshipping in secret, and the continuity was such that the hidden seed was to flourish in Herrnhut.

Comenius's contribution to education in England was, however, cut short by the Civil War in 1641. Further visits to Sweden and Holland (where he died) were more influential. The work of Comenius preserved the succession of the episcopacy, achieved through his son-in-law Peter Jablonsky. He in turn consecrated his son (and Comenius's grandson) Daniel Ernest Jablonsky. Daniel then consecrated David Nitschmann as the first Bishop of the Renewed Church in 1737.

The Moravians had a hard time during the second half of the seventeenth century, but help was at hand in a series of coincidences. Christian David, who was born in 1690, was diverted from his Catholic upbringing by the example of a number of Protestants imprisoned for their beliefs. While seeking work as a carpenter, David went to Görlitz in Silesia where he met a Lutheran pastor with whom he discussed his ideas. The pastor had a friend named Johann Rothe, who was studying theology, and the two became friends. Rothe was to become pastor in the village of Berthelsdorf.

When David returned to Moravia, he met some of the persecuted Christians and realised how much they needed somewhere to practise their religion properly. Meantime, a nobleman, Count

Nicholas von Zinzendorf, was beginning to sympathise with the Protestant cause. He had been deeply moved by a painting seen in Düsseldorf of Christ wearing the crown of thorns. An inscription below the picture read, 'I did this for you; what have you done for me?' This led the count to rededicate his life to Christ.

He had recently bought an estate at Berthelsdorf. It just happened that he met Rothe there, from whom he learned of the situation facing the Moravians, and expressed sympathy. Some of them came as refugees and settled on land on Zinzendorf's estate while he was away. In his absence, Baroness Gersdorf, Zinzendorf's maternal grandmother, put the refugees in the care of the estate agent, a man named Heiz. He it was who chose the location near to Hutberg, which translates as 'Watchman's Hill'. The name Herrnhut derives from this; it means 'The Lord's Watch'.

The refugees were soon able to start to build their settlement. The date of 17 June 1772 celebrates the felling of the first tree to provide building material, a date still acknowledged in the Moravian calendar. When Zinzendorf returned from his travels after some months and was heading for the village of Hennersdorf, where he had been cared for as a child by his grandmother, he noticed the lights from the newly erected buildings – his first sight of the new community which he made welcome.

Some early tensions in the growing body were perhaps inevitable. In an attempt to deal with these, Zinzendorf drew up a sequence of rules which all settlers had to accept, and presented this to them on 12 May 1727. Agreement was secured, and the count himself moved in to the settlement. He discussed the rules with the people, and this gave rise to 'The Brotherly Union & Compact'. The formal document was signed on 4 July, Christian David being one of the signatories. Shortly afterwards, in the library of the nearby town of Zittau, Zinzendorf discovered a copy of some of the writings of Comenius, including 'The Discipline of the Bohemian Brethren'. In reading this, he realised why the Brethren of the Old Bohemian Church, who were strongly represented in Herrnhut, had so readily agreed with his rules and happily signed them himself. He shared these findings with the people on 26 July.

Rothe, in his role as pastor of Berthelsdorf, had not taken

kindly to the new community, but the signing of the agreement caused him to change his position. He invited them to a communion service in the little village church on 13 August 1727, which was to be memorable indeed. Those present had an amazing experience, a kind of Pentecost, during which the men and women of various backgrounds suddenly became convinced of their 'oneness in Christ'. It was a 'baptism of the Spirit', which confirmed for them that they were indeed doing the will of God. The date is still part of the Moravian calendar.

After the service, they stayed together in small groups in various houses, to which the count sent food so that they could continue in prayer. Indeed, this continuous prayer-watch continued for a hundred years. In acknowledgement of the quincentenary of the Moravian Church in 1957, the Worldwide Unity re-established it, and it continues to this day, passing from one community of Moravians to another in an ongoing cycle.

One idea to foster fellowship among the new community was to give a daily 'watchword', a text from the Bible for reflection which was delivered to each house, at first by word of mouth but later printed. It was meant to be a uniting bond that each should meditate upon the same word from the Bible each day. For 1731, a sequence was published for the whole year, with these texts supplemented by verses quoted from hymns, and this has become a noted feature of Moravian life ever since. The edition for 2009 is the 279th. The Old Testament verses are drawn by lot from the same glass bowl as has been used since the first edition, and New Testament quotations and verses from hymns are then added by editors. The collection is translated into at least fifty languages and its readership extends well beyond the Moravian circles that create it. Most acts of worship and most meetings in the Moravian tradition will include reading the entry for the relevant day.

From this experience of 13 August, still celebrated today in Moravian prayer, came renewed acceptance of the old principles of government, discipline and doctrine. The line of the episcopate was also revived, forming a bond between the old and the new. The Moravian Church had found its soul again and soon began to flourish.

At the heart of their worship was an intense simplicity,

reflected in their buildings and their communities, and a deep respect for each individual person before God. Liturgy for them has always been seen only as an aid to worship and never as prescriptive. Indeed the early Methodist movement drew from, and incorporated, much of the Moravian tradition; like Methodism, it was never intended to become a separate denomination, but an encouragement to deeper spirituality within existing ecclesiastical bodies. In his book *The Exotic Plant*[3] Geoffrey Stead writes that Zinzendorf wanted to create 'an interdenominational movement in support of existing Protestant Churches'. In England the movement initially had more to do with the Church of England than it had with other elements in the evangelical revival.

One of their first initiatives in this new awakening was to establish Moravian missions, based on chance meetings by Zinzendorf when visiting the Danish court for the coronation of King Christian VI of Denmark in 1731. There the Count heard of the terrible conditions being endured by the slaves in the West Indies, and when he returned to Herrnhut the Moravians determined to do something about it. The work quickly developed its own momentum, and in the following year Moravian missionary work had begun; within eight years it had reached every quarter of the globe. Its first focus was to the black slaves on the other side of the Atlantic, and as many of the territories in which they found themselves were part of the British Empire, a Moravian agency was founded in London in 1735.

London was the recognised centre for travel, trade and commerce, and of course there were an increasing number of German residents in the city after the Hanoverian succession of 1714. There were also increasing numbers of Germans in the new communities in America. A number of Moravians had to await ships in London en route for their missionary work, Peter Boehler among them, and the agency centre was set up to meet their needs, with Zinzendorf's support. This became a Congregation in 1742, in Fetter Lane in the City of London. The premises suffered severe damage during the Second World War,

---

[3] Geoffrey and Margaret Stead, *The Exotic Plant: A History of the Moravian Church in Britain 1742-2000*, Peterborough, Epworth Press, 2003

and the name lives on, now associated with the Moravian chapel in Chelsea. It was in 1749 that the British Parliament recognised the Moravians as 'an ancient, Protestant, Episcopal Church'. They never grew to be particularly strong in this country; they worked to win souls for the Lord through evangelism, not to proselytise. It is important to note that, unlike many Churches, the Moravians never had a separate missionary society; they saw mission as integral to what they stood for.

The London Moravians quickly made a favourable impression and their reputation soon spread. Perhaps their most significant meeting was with John Wesley in 1735. Both he and his brother Charles had volunteered for service overseas, and they were sent to Savannah, Georgia, in America. It so happened that a group of Moravians was also making the journey in pursuit of their own missionary endeavours, and they spent time together on the ship; Benjamin Ingham and Charles Delamotte were among them. Some time elapsed before they could depart, during which time Wesley got to know them and was deeply impressed by their piety, industry and their attitude of total surrender to their faith. Indeed, soon after his arrival in Georgia in 1736, Wesley's confidence was undermined by some pertinent questioning by a Moravian pastor as to the depth of his conviction that Christ was his Saviour.

It was after his return from America that Wesley met Peter Boehler, and their shared conversations were important. These came during a period of uncertainty for Wesley, who even questioned whether he should go on preaching. Boehler's advice (in March 1738) was: 'Preach faith until you have it, and then, because you have it, you will preach faith.' A number of meetings took place, and after Boehler left for Carolina in May 1738 he wrote to Wesley. It was on 24 May that he experienced his heart 'strangely warmed' at the meeting in Aldersgate Street; this he later described as his conversion.

Wesley visited Herrnhut for twelve days in the summer of 1738. He met Count Nicholas von Zinzendorf and shared in the Moravians' daily worship. He would have loved to spend more time there, but this was his only visit. Following his return to England, Wesley continued to associate with the Moravians, not least through his friendship with Br Peter Boehler, to whom he now owed much in his journey of faith. Later he adopted many of the Moravian practices into what became Methodism: using hymnody to teach theology, for example.

Some tensions developed, not least between Wesley and the young Philip Molther, and by 1740 Wesley had separated from his friendship with these Moravian brothers. Br Molther became a bishop of the Unity in 1775 during his ministry in Bedford (1766–81); he is interred in the burial ground behind the church. Wesley himself visited Bedford again in 1788 and lodged with the Moravian George Livius at Grove House, which stood on the site between St Cuthbert's Street and The Grove; Wesley regarded it as 'the best house by far in the town'. Maybe this hospitality helped him to conclude that 'as all disputes are at an end, there is great reason to hope that the work of God will increase here also'. Zinzendorf himself spent the years 1750–55 in London. He purchased a fine town house, Lindsey House, in Cheyne Walk, Chelsea, which after renovation became for two years the international headquarters of the Moravian Church. He lived there himself from 1753 until his return to Germany in 1755.

At the final services at St Luke's, the Advent Star was displayed, albeit a little early! It has a very special place in Moravian tradition. The multi-pointed Advent Star is a three-dimensional construction made from elongated pyramids of paper and illuminated from within by a low-wattage bulb. It usually has twenty-five points, of which seventeen have a square base and eight are triangular. Larger ones can be found with 120 points, measuring up to five feet across. They were first made in about 1850 in evening handicraft lessons at Niesky in eastern Germany; by 1880 Peter Verbeek had set up a small cottage industry making them. His son Harry then established a factory in Herrnhut. This was re-established after the Second World War and the stars manufactured there serve both the domestic and the export markets. They are set up in Moravian Churches, and even in homes, from Advent Sunday over Christmas until Epiphany (6 January) which acknowledges the visit of the Magi. The stars proclaim a threefold message:

- They bear witness to the greatness of God the Creator who made the stars (Genesis 1:16) to be uncountable (Genesis 15:5) and differing in splendour (1 Corinthians 15:41), and the morning stars which sang together when the Lord laid the earth's foundations (Job 38:7);

- They represent the star which went before the Wise Men from the east until they reached Bethlehem where 'it came and stood over where the young child was. When they saw the star, they rejoiced'. Approaching the infant Jesus, 'they fell down and worshipped him; and when they had opened their treasures they presented unto him gifts: gold, frankincense and myrrh' (Matthew 2:9–11);

- They point to the star that 'shall come out of Jacob' (Numbers 24:17), a prophecy that was fulfilled in Jesus who said of himself: 'I am the root and the offspring of David, and the bright and morning star' (Revelation 22:16).

The ancient symbol of the Moravian Church is the Lamb and Flag, drawn from biblical verses. The Lamb is shown as walking with the dexter forepaw raised, and carrying a resurrection cross, from which is suspended a triumphal banner. It symbolises the verse from John 1:29, when Jesus is described as 'the Lamb of God that takes away the sin of the world'. The Moravian historian William Reichel describes it thus:

> It blends the prophetic, the historic and the apocalyptic, pointing to the Lamb without blemish, to the Paschal Lamb, to the Lamb of God that takes away the sin of the world, to the Lamb slain before the foundation of the world and to the Lamb that shall overcome, being Lord of Lords and King of Kings. [4]

It was adopted from the very earliest days of the Unitas Fratrum, appearing on many books and documents of the Church and used on Episcopal seals. It has become the official insignia of the Moravian Church. Its Latin motto, *Vicit agnus noster – eum*

---

[4] William Reichel, *Memorials of the Moravian Church*, Philadelphia, J B Lippincott & Co., 1870

sequamur, means 'Our Lamb has conquered – let us follow him.'

Another powerful visual symbol that owes its origins to the Moravian Church is the Christingle. It is first mentioned in the congregational diary of the Church at Marienborn in Germany on 20 December 1747. The minister, John de Watteville, used hymns and verses that the children had written and went on to explain what happiness had come to people through the birth of Jesus, 'who had kindled in each little heart a flame which ever keeps burning to their joy and happiness'. To help the children remember this, each was given a lighted wax candle with a red ribbon 'which occasioned in great and small a happy children's joy'. The service ended with the prayer: 'Lord Jesus, kindle a flame in these dear children's hearts that theirs like thine become.' The diary concludes: 'hereupon the children went full of joy with their little lighted candles to their rooms and so went glad and happy to bed.' Subsequently the idea was followed in many parts of the world and was developed into what we know today with its various symbolic parts:

- The orange, representing the world;
- The white ruff: purity;
- The goose quill (split into six spikes): birds of the air and beasts of the field;
- Almonds and raisins (on the spikes): fruits of the earth;
- The red ribbon (tied round the candle): the blood of Jesus;
- The white candle: Christ, the Light of the World.

The Christingle Service is traditionally held on Christmas Eve. In the service the child is placed at the very heart of all that is done, just as the Christ Child is at the centre of the festival. After carols and readings in the darkened church, each child receives a Christingle, its candle alight, and they all process round the church to show the coming of the light – a magical moment to herald Christmas. The old Moravian carol brings the service to its end:

Morning Star, O cheering sight!
Ere thou camst, how dark earth's night.
Jesus mine, in me shine,
Fill my heart with light divine.

Another important element of Moravian tradition is the Love-feast. It originated in apostolic times when, following the day of Pentecost, believers met and broke bread together as a sign of their unity. The idea was resurrected in Herrnhut when small groups of people met in each other's homes to talk about their spiritual experiences, especially after what had been shared in the Spirit at Berthelsdorf. Zinzendorf realised the potential value of maintaining this, and encouraged the practice whenever new settlements were founded. The Lovefeast is still enjoyed on special occasions. The Lovefeast cup is not consecrated, but would sometimes precede the sacrament of the Lord's Supper, and would provide opportunity for sharing news. It touches on a sense of intimacy, of brotherhood and deep fellowship with one another. Hymns and prayers are shared, and then tea and buns (sometimes containing currants!) are distributed. If possible the ladies wear traditional Moravian dress, modelled on the costume of the eighteenth century. The presiding minister then reads the watchword for the day, and the tea and buns are enjoyed while the minister gives the address. Hymn verses are sung, the cups gathered, an offering taken, and the feast ends with the Right Hand of Fellowship shared with each other. Sometimes at the end of a formal meeting, the Cup of Covenant is shared, symbolising imminent departure. It was first used in Herrnhut to bless the departure of a brother to the mission field in 1729, but is used more generally now, to symbolise the sense of fellowship and brotherhood.

Not all these traditional elements have been observed in more recent years at St Luke's, but reference to them serves to empha-sise again the close community of love that develops through the sharing of such practices. One record refers to the practice of the minister who, at the end of the service, would walk slowly down the aisle, shaking hands with the person nearest to him, who would then shake hands with his neighbour and so on until the entire congregation had shared in this act of togetherness. The value of such gestures lies ultimately in faith, but it can be endlessly enriched when that faith is underlined by meaningful practice. Today this tradition is confused with the Sharing of the Peace in many churches. Maintaining such practices with others at functions and in worship brings an immediate reality to the sense of family relationship within the fellowship of the Church. This quickly transcends such difficulties as might be encountered elsewhere, even of nationality, language and colour. Unlike so much of what is emphasised in society today, such traditional devices are simple, very meaningful and honed by years of loving appreciation. Much can be learned from this...

The Moravians in Bedford

When an outbreak of smallpox affected Bedford in 1738–9, help
was sought, and found, among the early Moravian community in
London. An invitation to help was issued by Jacob Rogers, a
curate at St Paul's, to Charles Delamotte and Benjamin Ingham,
helped by Francis Okely. The help was willingly given, and as a
result a Society was soon formed which met in a barn behind the
Okely home (5–7 High Street). Rogers himself was persuaded,
and became the first Moravian minister, starting to preach in his
new style on St Peter's Green. Despite a wealth of records there is
some confusion over the details of the original foundation: one
account claims that in 1742 there were 'forty-two awakened
souls'; 1745 is acknowledged as the starting point of the work in
Bedford, the date when they were recognised as a congregation.
Until this happened, the members had to travel to London to
receive communion, a journey which took a day and a half by
stagecoach.

In these early days, those associating themselves with this
work were often bullied, not least because of their 'foreign' name.
They acquired land on the edge of the town centre in St Peter's
Street where Br Boehler consecrated the chapel and the burial
ground in 1751. In true Moravian tradition, all gravestones were
of a uniform size and laid flat, for all are equal in the sight of God.
The church, originally known as the Bedford Congregation, was
at the centre, with the Single Sisters' House to the west
(24 St Peter's Street) where the women (forty-five in the mid-
nineteenth century) earned a living through needlework and
embroidery. J H Matthiason's *Bedford and its Environs* of 1831
reported that the Single Sisters 'occupy themselves in various
species of needle and other useful and ornamental work, which
produces a considerable income for the benefit of the institution
and its parent interests, the work being universally admired and
generally sold at a high price.'

The Brothers' House was to the east (this later became the minister's manse) where they earned their living by baking bread. The bakery was later converted into a Sunday school, also in 1801. The Sisters would come into church from the west side, wearing bonnets with ribbons to indicate their marital status: juveniles were red, pink for the single, blue for the married, white for the widowed. The Brothers would enter from the east, wearing cloaks with white cowls (the two side aisles marked the division). The Brothers later moved to a larger building behind the original settlement, which later served as the Moravian Ladies' School. There was once a cottage in front of the Sisters' House (it was demolished in 1872) where Zinzendorf stayed on his visit to Bedford in 1757 on the occasion of the laying of the foundation stone of the Sisters' House; the date, 26 May, was the count's birthday. The cottage was once occupied by a greengrocer and had a kitchen garden; one old account records that 'the vision did not remind one of Eden, nor the odour of Araby'. Mercifully, it adds, 'all that has changed'. The long sweep of Georgian facades on St Peter's Street is still a significant feature of the townscape, and hopefully will remain so in the new situation.

The work of the Moravians quickly spread throughout the district, and at one stage there were more than twenty chapels or preaching houses in the Bedford group, all depicted in the well-known etching by John England of 1886; the Bedford buildings are based on drawings by Bradford Rudge who died in 1885. The engraving, which shows the original chapel and its adjoining buildings, is from earlier than 1864, perhaps a lithograph of c.1850. Copies of these prints have been given to the Bedford Museum: pictured are establishments at Riseley, Pertenhall, Kimbolton, Keysoe, Great Staughton and, to the south of Bedford, at Silsoe. The picture of the Moravian Ladies' School bears the legend 'sketched by moonlight, February 27 1886', suggesting a certain furtiveness. It may be that the artist simply ran out of time after working on several sketches during the day. A small community at Northampton, consecrated in June 1770, was serviced from Bedford.

The Rev. Philip Henry Molther was prominent in those early days as noted. Another significant figure was William Foster

(1722–68). He and his brother Joseph owned land in Bedford and also in Jamaica, and he invited the Moravians to minister on their plantations there. This offered a convenient link with the mission work in those islands already under way.

The Bradford Rudge print of the St Luke's site of 1851
with acknowledgement to the Cecil Higgins Art Gallery, Bedford

The original chapel of 1751 was replaced and enlarged by a second one in 1795. This has been known to cause confusion, in that no pictures are known to exist of the very first building – it is the second one that is illustrated after 1795. By the middle of the nineteenth century, even this was considered inadequate, and it took time for suitable enlargement plans to be accepted. The present building, in a Victorian Italianate style designed by James Horsford, was officially opened on 9 March 1865; it had cost £2,000. During the laying of the foundation stone in June 1864 part of the roof of the old chapel fell among the crowd, injuring Sr Martha Trapp, a member of a distinguished Moravian family.

To acknowledge the significance of what had been achieved, the Moravian Synod met here in 1863; one of the major decisions was to launch *The Moravian Messenger*, described as 'a magazine of the Church of the United Brethren' to enable the members to keep abreast of the development of ideas and thinking more widely, together with reports of progress. From 1994 to 2008 the magazine was edited by the Rev. Fred Linyard, who had been minister at St Luke's in the 1950s.

Later the chapel was further enlarged to the north to accommodate the new organ (see later chapter). The new apse provided space for the choir stalls and for the screen, the one element from the original organ of 1715 to have survived into the modern period. These additional buildings intruded into the burial ground, but the original God's Acre remained. Its plants and evergreens made it, according to one report, 'suggestive of life and incorruption'. When Bedford's municipal cemetery was opened in 1855, it was ordered by the Privy Council (no less) that no further burials should be made in churchyards. Some Moravian burials took place there after 1875; the last burial in the original burial ground being enacted in 1917, although cremated remains were occasionally accepted since then.

To mark the Church's 150th anniversary in 1895, a new congregation was established in Queen's Park; this community was extending to the west of the railway to serve Bedford's growing industrial plant. W H Allen had purchased some twenty acres of land from the Whitbread family in 1893, and established his engineering works there in the following year. This period was perhaps the high point of Moravian influence within the town, when Bishop Evelyn Hasse was the minister. It is to his memory that the Lutyens panels displaying the Ten Commandments on the eastern wall are dedicated.

On 9 March two services were held in the church, each with sermons from Moravian Bishops, Br C E Sutcliffe in the morning and Br Blandford in the evening. The foundation stones of the Queen's Park Chapel were laid the following day, with Sir Frederick Howard JP speaking of his family's long connection with the Unity. The Church School at Queen's Park was opened in August of that year; board schools were not set up there by the local authority until 1899. The opening of this church coincided with the Provincial Synod being held in Bedford. In fact, by 1900

Bedford had one of the largest congregations in the country, second only to Fulneck. It was at this time that the church took the name of St Peter's to distinguish it from the Queen's Park congregation.

The Moravian Ladies' School was a prominent feature of the life of the Church from 1801 until 1914; indeed the venture into private boarding schools was for many years very profitable and may have saved the Church nationally from financial disaster. The school in St Peter's Street offered 'Religious Teaching and Training on Pure Evangelical Lines', and among its attributes were a gymnasium, a tennis court and 'open and covered playgrounds'. The Elementary Education Act of 1870 began a much-needed improvement to schools generally, prompted partly by the increasing strength of denominational schools that were thought to be exclusive. The Education Act of 1902 established local education authorities (LEAs), which were initially the county councils, and they raised an education rate. This Act was opposed by many Nonconformists, who felt that their rates were helping to fund Church of England schools. However, some improvements at secondary level were achieved. In Bedford the onward march of the Bedford Charity (Harpur Trust) schools was also making an impact.

Bishop Hasse of Bedford had the awesome task of addressing the Fairfield Synod in 1914, just as the First World War was starting, and the known links of the Moravian Church with Germany proved to be something of an encumbrance. The Moravian Ladies' School as such contracted but continued as a private institution for a few more years under Mrs Starling, until it finally closed in 1921. Their original building became part of Bedford School (Howard Building), which was named after the Trust's chairman Geoffrey Howard. It was later extended under the direction of the distinguished architect Sir Albert Richardson.

After the Great War, the standing of the Moravian Church began to decline. Its foreign name and strong German associations did it no favours. As the town grew, the Methodist Church was also gaining in strength. The Moravians' influence reduced still further after the Second World War, but the national Synod was again held at Bedford in 1949. This was the setting for the start of an initiative that led to the formation of the Moravian Women's Auxiliary (later Association). Sr Eileen Shawe visited the United States, where such activities were already under way, and the initiative was raised at Synod. A provincial committee explored the suggestion and meetings began in January 1950. The standing of St Luke's was given new impetus with the coming of the Presbyterian Church in 1952 when, as shown in a later chapter, a number of further initiatives began to reach out into society.

In his presentation, the first of the four evenings to reflect this church's heritage, Bishop John McOwat drew parallels between his own personal pilgrimage and the history of the Moravian Church he serves. He sketched the story of how the Moravians had reached their present position, and indeed of his own journey, from early training for the ministry, his call to serve in Jamaica and later in this country both in pastoral care and in administration, leading to his election as Bishop in 2002. He went on to outline the founding beliefs, and spoke of Moravian Church worship and practice. He reminded his listeners of the three centres of Moravian life: Christ, the Bible, and People. These were set in congregational life, which was followed to deepen fellowship and avoid any kind of discrimination. It served, if anything, to emphasise the sadness of what would be lost when St Luke's United Church finally closed.

The Presbyterian Heritage

The Presbyterian Church arose out of the turmoil of the Reformation in the sixteenth and seventeenth centuries. The word 'arose' is used deliberately, for it was not seen as an innovation; rather as a return to the values of the early Church as recorded in the pages of the New Testament. The modern understanding of this is based on the teachings of John Calvin (1509–64). His work is thought to have started in Geneva in 1536. The word 'Presbyterian' derives from that, its origins being in the Greek word *presbyteros*, meaning a church leader, and was certainly in common usage in Scotland by the middle of the seventeenth century.

One of the principal figures in the early path towards this model of churchmanship was the reformer John Knox (1513–72). He had been appointed chaplain to the young King Edward VI in 1551 and worked on the revision of the second version of the Book of Common Prayer. When Mary ascended the throne in 1556 and set about re-establishing the Catholic faith, Knox went to the continent and was appointed to the English Church in Geneva. After Mary's death, he returned to Scotland to lead the reforming movement there. He was instrumental in drawing up the Scottish Confession, which was adopted by the Scottish Parliament in 1560.

Another leading figure, Thomas Cartwright, used his position as Professor of Divinity at Cambridge to urge a simpler structure of Church governance, which saw the church as consisting of a pastor and a congregation who would arrange their life together; there was no need for episcopal oversight or authority. Indeed the whole concept of society was being questioned, with the vested interests of the rich and powerful being challenged. Cromwell's victory in the Civil War gave some hope to a permanent change in society, but this was short-lived: the restoration of the monarchy in 1660 soon re-established the status quo.

The Presbyterian Church derives essentially from the Westminster Confession, which was approved by Parliament in 1648. It grew out of the deliberations which began in 1643 and took three years. Thirty lay-assessors and 121 members of the clergy met in Westminster Abbey to revise the thirty-nine Articles of the Church of England. It was confirmed by the Long Parliament in 1648. Agreement was sought between the English and Scottish Parliaments in 1643 in the form of a Solemn League and Covenant. This set out to establish the Presbyterian Church of Scotland, to reform the Church of England and to achieve the unity of all churches in Britain. The Presbyterians sought to include as Christians all who had been baptised and who lived in society. The Independents would not agree; they accepted as members only those who had made a public declaration of faith, and as they grew in influence, further progress towards unity in England was not possible. After much deliberation, these findings were accepted in Scotland, and were allowed to continue as long as they caused no disturbance of the peace.

Two Catechisms were defined, the Larger and the Smaller. The Smaller is the better known, not least because of its opening question: 'What is the chief end of Man? Man's chief end is to glorify God and to enjoy him for ever.' The Confession was quickly ratified by the Church of Scotland, and soon came to be accepted as the definitive statement of Presbyterianism in the English-speaking world. The Act of Uniformity of 1662 demanded that all priests taking public worship should conform to the Book of Common Prayer. Further restrictions were introduced by legislation. Many would not conform, and some 1,600 were ejected from office on 24 August, the Feast of St Bartholomew.

Life became increasingly difficult for such ministers, especially after the Conventicle Act of 1664, which declared that any meeting of more than five people (in addition to those within the household) for worship other than prescribed in the Book of Common Prayer was illegal. In the following year came the Five Mile Act, which banned those clergy and ministers who refused to accept the terms of the Act of Uniformity from teaching, preaching or even coming within five miles of the place where they had previously ministered unless they promised not to challenge the laws of the state. It was also decreed that any place of worship not accepting state legislation had to be at least fifty yards from the public highway.

All dissenting churches struggled against these laws until, with the death of James II and the succession to the throne of William and Mary in 1689, the Act of Toleration enabled a more sensible regulation of the dissenting traditions (Baptists, Congregationalists and Quakers), with Presbyterians too. They were finally established in Scotland in 1690, but progress was less marked in England owing to the rapid spread of Methodism during the eighteenth century. The growth of the Presbyterian Church was helped by the repeal of some of the Test Acts (which restricted many occupations to those who were Anglican communicants) in 1828. The rapid expansion of many English towns and cities in what became known as the Industrial Revolution encouraged large numbers of people from Scotland and Ireland to move to England looking for work. This was especially notable in the cotton and woollen mills of Lancashire and Yorkshire. In 1844 this encouraged the formation of the Presbyterian Church in England, and this was enlarged in 1876 to form the Presbyterian Church of England with more than 250 member churches.

In brief, the main elements of the Presbyterian Church include, firstly, the belief that each and every person is equal in the sight of God, a belief founded on biblical principles and, of course, one shared with the Moravians. The only head of the Church is Jesus Christ himself, and the attributes of the Church derive from the indwelling of the Holy Spirit in each and every person. Thus all are equal, ordained ministers and people, each of whom can receive and display spiritual qualities. The word *presbyter*, in the Greek of the Acts of the Apostles, is used to define those appointed to oversee the work of the local congregations in those churches founded by St Paul.

There was another level of oversight by a more senior figure; the Greek word is *episcope*, meaning a bishop. The position of bishop grew in significance after the second century, when such figures were given a controlling authority to maintain the work of the Church within accepted guidelines. Episcopacy was never accepted in Presbyterian churchmanship. Those accepted as presbyters became priests, assisted by deacons who could administer some lesser services, based on the calling of the seven deacons in Acts 6. All these structures acknowledged the call in 1 Corinthians 14:40, that 'everything should be done decently and in order.'

The Presbyterian Church is governed by these principles laid down in the New Testament, and is administered by councils of ministers and elected and ordained elders meeting together in the session – another word for the people being together. Calvin struggled to find an acceptable balance between not leaving authority in any single pair of hands and needing to trust the collective wisdom of shared oversight. A form of church government evolved known as conciliar ecclesiology, which means government through councils. The lowest is the Kirk Session, which consists of the members of the local church with their elders and minister. All ministers are equal in status, so there are no bishops and no hierarchy. The session or meeting is responsible for the call of a minister and for the pastoral welfare of the members of the church; each enjoyed the services of a session clerk, responsible for the proper conduct of the allocated duties. Membership of the Church belongs to those who, having been baptised, have openly declared their faith in Jesus Christ as Lord before the congregation.

The local church would ordain certain members to the eldership to form a council responsible for local order; these members would form a court (which met in the Court Room). Short meetings might be held before worship to exchange news and offer prayer; they were formally structured and minuted. Each elder would be responsible for the regular visitation of church members and adherents in a defined district.

Representatives of each local church would meet as a district or presbytery; this meeting had oversight of and jurisdiction over particular areas, and also oversaw the welfare of local congregations. The presbytery had responsibility for the ordination of ministers and would confirm their appointment. These districts in turn would gather in areas known as a synod, which again had responsibility for the oversight and ordering of the administration of the churches in its wider area. Representatives were then appointed to the General Assembly, the ultimate governing body which would meet annually to define the framework in which the work of the churches would proceed. The presiding officer, the moderator, was usually elected and appointed for one year.

Presbyterian worship has traditionally been simple and straightforward. All that happens is subject to the authority of the Word of God in the Bible, another idea shared with the Moravians. The congregation stands as the Bible is carried in at the start of the service and placed on the lectern, its open pages facing them. It remains in position throughout the service and is carried out at the end, the minister following; this shows that he or she is subject to its authority. It demonstrates, according to F G Healey, 'in a symbolic way that the Scriptures are the Church's chief standard of faith and duty and the chief means whereby the living Word of God can be heard today.' This goes back to Calvin's assertion in his *Institutes* (I.7:4–5): 'Our conviction of the truth of Scripture must be derived from a higher source than human conjectures, judgements or reasons, namely the secret testimony of the Spirit.'

There is no fixed liturgy as such, but the service follows a pattern as set out in the Book of Order, with prayers, psalms (often metrical versions), readings from the Bible and the sermon being interspersed with hymns. The Lord's Supper (or Holy Communion) is not usually administered very often; traditionally it was only held once a quarter. It holds a very special place in Presbyterian practice, for which preparatory visits are made by the elders to the homes of those members expecting to participate.

One amusing afterthought to this survey: someone within the Church worked out an anagram of the word Presbyterian, and found 'Best in Prayer'. The experience of many would confirm this!

The Presbyterians in Bedford

There are few historical references to Presbyterians in Bedford-shire in the seventeenth century, but numbers were never very great. Licences for places of worship were applied for in Cardington among other places, and there was a small congregation in Sharnbrook in the 1760s. There had been a significant presence of people of Scottish descent in Bedford for some time, but this increased at the outset of the First World War in 1914, when some 20,000 Scottish soldiers were billeted in the town for basic training before going to the front. They were drawn from the 51st Highland Division, whose regiments included the Gordon, Cameron and Argyll & Sutherland Highlanders. They were away from their homelands for the first time, but found a warm reception in the town. The churches were prominent among the many organisations that put on events for them and helped to make them welcome. Many of the soldiers were ill prepared for the effects of such childhood diseases as measles, and with the onset of autumn and winter many of them succumbed; for some it proved fatal. A dignified part of the cemetery in Foster Hill Road contains the graves of thirty-three, and their memory is honoured each year by a separate act of Remembrance on the first Sunday of November.

It may surprise some to learn that the modern history of the Presbyterian Church in Bedford only begins during the Second World War. It started as a church extension project in 1942. The first members started to meet in the Assembly Rooms and then in St Cuthbert's Hall, before moving to the Conduit Rooms in Conduit Road. This made possible regular Sunday services and even the start of the Sunday school. Recognition as a congregation came in 1946 and numbers increased to 150. A part-time minister was appointed, a manse purchased in Warwick Avenue and a plot of land for a church acquired in Dynevor Road. Meantime, the hall premises were proving quite inadequate for the growing numbers. In 1949 the Rev. David Davies was appointed full-time to minister to the 250 members and sixty children; he was a respected preacher and teacher. He became unwell, and moved to warmer climes in South Africa, where he conducted a successful ministry. A choir was formed, which initially met for practice in members' homes. As support continued to increase rapidly, thoughts soon turned to the building of a church.

Post-war restrictions on building new churches meant that their application was turned down. An article by the Rev. George A Harding, the first Presbyterian minister of this church, in preparation for a forthcoming Synod in 1964, sketched these early days in the town in the style of the Acts of the Apostles:

> So they came to Bedford and formed a congregation. They worshipped at the Conduit Rooms, but were prevented by the Holy Spirit from staying there. They were in high hopes of building their Church on a reserved site, but the Spirit of Jesus said, No. They settled in another hall, but the Spirit intervened and said, Seek elsewhere! So they came to St Peter's (the name for this site at the time), and it was here that together Moravians and Presbyterians had their vision: Remain no more two. Become one.

This move, dating from 1952, was one of the first significant ecumenical initiatives in the town.

Cooperation between the two congregations grew as they seemed to get on with each other. Historically some of the very first Moravians in England were drawn from Presbyterian sources. The Moravian Church in Bedford at the time had only fifty members, and invited the Presbyterians to come and share in worship and use the facilities for the weeknight activities that were expanding too. For a time each maintained their organisations separately, but Sunday worship was shared; children's work and that of the choirs was united from the start. For a time the church had the luxury of two ministers and two manses, the second one being at 83 Goldington Road.

The North London Presbytery and the Moravian Church explored the potential for closer union from 1956; it was established in 1960. Both gave grants, which led to the building of the first hall in 1961. This was decorated by volunteers. Over two years considerable work was done on the gardens; the former burial ground was levelled and reseeded and a number of trees were felled. The church was also redecorated, and renovation work started on the organ, which took over two years.

The combined forces of the united congregations made quite an impact. Activities included Brownies, Girl Guides, two meetings for women, and committees for raising funds for missionary work both at home and overseas. A youth council sought to coordinate efforts in that age group. Some members would meet for poetry readings. A drama group was established, which quickly built up quite a reputation and its productions could fill the Civic Theatre twice a year with a repertory that included Noel Coward's *Blithe Spirit* and work by Agatha Christie. A Scottish dancing group was another initiative which reached high standards: on one occasion they were invited to dance at a function in the Dorchester Hotel in London in the presence of HRH The Princess Margaret. Their hopes were strong, but this was the time when numbers in church life overall began to diminish. It was reported that in these four years, a total of 150 adults and children had left Presbyterian churches in the district. It was a trend that was sadly to continue.

One successful element of life in these years was undoubtedly the Presbyterian Women's Guild, which was already flourishing by 1951. There were clear obligations laid on members to the Church 'to try to fulfil our duties with dignity and loyalty … only by the closest cooperation between Church and Guild can we hope to further our Father's Kingdom here on earth'. Their programme consisted of the usual round of speakers and demon-strations, together with visits to local factories and other organisations engaged in social questions. Sometimes a coach was hired to travel further afield to visit Windsor, Stratford and Felixstowe, and to the cathedrals of Ely and Worcester. They also met for dinners and theatre trips. One member of the Bedford Church, Mrs Richards, was appointed President of the Women's Federation of the Free Church Federal Council in 1959.

One family was to take a prominent part in the life of the church: the Clarkes. Major Cecil Vandepeer Clarke MC, commonly known as Nobby, was an ordained elder of the Presbyterian Church, and described as 'a man of many interests'. He had served in the First World War with the Staffordshire Regiment, and in the Second as a member of the Intelligence Corps (Special Operations). He was a member of Bedford Borough Council for many years, initially for Labour but later as a Liberal. In 1950 he was appointed as a magistrate. Major Clarke devised a limpet mine for attacking enemy shipping, and tales abound of the effects of his experiments with aniseed which would often explode quite unexpectedly, probably on the mantelpiece in the family home. This work is referred to in Stephen Bunker's *The Spy Capital of Britain: Bedfordshire's Secret War, 1939–1945*[5] published in 2007.

After the war he worked with the Low-Loading Trailer Co. Ltd in Dean Street; this had been founded in 1926 in Tavistock Street, and sold to J Crawley & Sons in 1948. His Christian principles led him to take part in the anti-nuclear protests, for which he was arrested on at least one occasion – it took several police officers to carry him away!

Various members of the family were deeply involved in so many aspects of church life, holding various offices, contributing to the music and drama and to the rebuilding work on the organ. David Clarke entered the Presbyterian ministry and served in several pastorates during his thirty-five years as a minister. John Clarke, another son, was the architect for the hall and kitchen. A third son, Roger, sadly died after a shortened career in the ministry of the Church of Scotland. Mrs Kenny Clarke contributed hugely to many different aspects of church life in the choir, as church secretary, in the Guild, with fundraising, as secretary to the Free Church Council. She died in December 2004, just short of her 102nd birthday.

In the second of the two presentation evenings, the Rev. Dr Alan Sell outlined the history of the Presbyterian Church, and also explored the relationship between what was essentially an English Presbyterian church in Bedford but which echoed Scottish patterns. There had been many disagreements in the

[5] Stephen Bunker, *The Spy Capital of Britain: Bedford's Secret War, 1939–45*, Bedford Chronicles, 2007

development of the Presbyterian traditions, not only over structures but also over the doctrine of the Trinity. Relationships between Church and State had also led to differences of emphasis in the two countries. By the end of the eighteenth century, most of the old English Presbyterian churches had become either Congregational or Unitarian. The nineteenth-century influx of various Presbyterian hues led to the formation of the Presbyterian Church of England in 1876. This body stood alongside other nonconformist churches in the Free Church Federal Council, and in 1972 it united with the majority of English and English-speaking Welsh Congregational churches to form the United Reformed Church. The Presbyterians had played a significant if short-lived role in the life of Bedford's churches.

The Congregational Heritage

Throughout much of the history of the English Churches since the Reformation, the Congregationalists have worked in parallel with the Presbyterians. Their concept of 'church' is based on the idea of the freedom of each local congregation independently to determine its own life according to local circumstances. This is still the case, although there are nationally accepted guidelines within which such an approach operates. An essential difference between the Congregational and Presbyterian Churches lies in the absence of set forms of liturgy, emphasising the freedom of extempore prayer. The Congregational Church published in 1959 a volume that was carefully entitled 'A Book of Services and Prayers'; the introduction stated clearly that 'it is neither designed nor intended to be used as a book of common prayer … its purpose is to provide guidance'.[6] It was felt that imposing any structure of worship would equate a liturgy with Scripture, and this would infringe their liberty. Indeed it is a principle that a Christian is answerable directly to Christ as Lord, without requiring any intervention of a priest or of state control.

The movement began in the 1550s, when those who had gained access to the Bible in English read in its pages of a very different kind of church structure from what they had experienced. They started to meet as house-groups to read and interpret the Word of God, and to share in Holy Communion with each other. This gained momentum during the reign of Elizabeth I but attracted opposition. Hearing of developments in the Netherlands, especially after the defeat of the Spanish forces of Philip II under the Duke of Alva, many fled there, especially to Leyden. It was from there that the Pilgrim Fathers sailed in the *Mayflower* in 1620, calling in at Southampton and Plymouth before crossing the Atlantic to found Plymouth, Massachusetts.

---

[6] *A Book of Services and Prayers*, London, Independent Press Ltd., 1959

These pioneer Christian settlers had enormous influence in the early days of setting up the American colonies.

The Independents (as they came to be known) supported Cromwell and went along with the Westminster Confession to some extent; they did not want to accept the structures proposed within it and defined their own principles in the Savoy Declaration of 1658, so called because the 120 representatives of Churches met in the Chapel of the Savoy in London. It contained echoes of the Westminster Confession but also declared the principle of having the power to determine policy vested in individual congregations. Some wanted to go even further and create a style of life quite separate from the rest of the community. These were called Separatists, which differentiated them from the similar style of the early Presbyterians, who would still have gone along with the parish system of the Church of England. Under the terms of the Act of Uniformity, they were declared to be Nonconformists and treated as being outside the law.

Congregationalism echoes the thought of Calvin, but is more loosely interpreted. The core belief is that the presence of Christ can be found in any fellowship that meets in his name. Each church is governed by the church meeting, which has the task of finding the mind of Christ for each such community. The church meeting is made up of those people admitted to membership of the congregation by a public declaration of their faith in Jesus Christ as Saviour and Lord. Members are drawn or gathered together because of their common understanding and not because of where they live; hence the idea of a 'gathered' church rather than a defined parish. Ministers are appointed by the church meeting and answerable to them. Their authority is based only on relationships and not on status or structures of authority. This form of church government proved to be important in shaping the development of national politics in our parliamentary democracy, a legacy of the support for Cromwell and Parliament during the struggles of the English Civil War.

The steady growth of the Independent Church continued during the eighteenth century. Isaac Watts and Philip Doddridge made significant contributions, not least through hymnody, as did George Whitefield. Indeed the early development of hymns was one of the most significant contributions made by Congregation-alism. The evangelical revival and the rapid growth of Methodism increased the standing of the Nonconformist traditions in general. One important development was the founding, in 1732, of the Protestant Dissenting Ministers and Deputies. This drew together the ministers from the Congregational, Presbyterian and Baptist churches within twelve miles of the cities of London and Westminster (there were 167) and their appointed deputies. These ministers led the fight against the Corporation and Test Acts, which continued to restrict the civil rights of Noncon-formists in society: a number of positions in government, the civil service, the universities and the army still required the holder to receive Holy Communion regularly according to the Book of Common Prayer as a condition of such employment.

The organisation of the Protestant Dissenting Ministers and Deputies arose from the varied receptions accorded to them by successive monarchs. When William III arrived in London in 1688, he was greeted by ninety Nonconformist ministers. When Queen Anne succeeded to the throne in 1702, ten went to the palace to assure her of their loyalty, but they were 'ungraciously' received. George II was greeted on his succession in 1727. By 1732, concerned about 'the visible decay of serious and practical religion' (among other matters) this group of leading ministers began a long struggle. A later Home Secretary, Sir Robert Peel, helped to establish the Right of Approach to the throne. Some forty organisations have this right, and the Protestant Dissenting Ministers and Deputies come fourth in priority after the General Synod of the Church of England and the universities of Oxford and Cambridge. It is a consequence of this that at each General Assembly of the United Reformed Church, the Loyal Address to the Queen is made.

One further important date is 1792, which saw the founding of the Baptist Missionary Society. This set a precedent that was followed up by the founding of the London Missionary Society by Congregationalists in 1795. Early in the nineteenth century, it was thought there ought to be some effort in offering mission to our own people, and so the Home Missionary Society was formed in 1819. This helped to support ministers in congregations that otherwise could not have been sustained. Congregationalists began to see the need to keep in touch with other Christians of similar persuasion on a wider basis, and to this end they grouped themselves into associations based loosely on counties. In 1832 this led to the founding of the Congregational Union of England and Wales, with their central headquarters in Memorial Hall in Farringdon Street in the City of London. This was built on part of the site of the ancient Fleet Prison, in which a number of early Independents had been held, and indeed from whence some were led to the scaffold! Ultimate authority for the Congregational Church was vested in the annual Assembly, on which each congregation could be represented, making up a truly representative national body. Towards the end of the nineteenth century, a significant milestone was reached with the founding of Mansfield College Oxford to train students for the Congregational ministry. Westminster College Cambridge (the writer's college) was also founded for the parallel path to ministry in the Presbyterian Church.

The Congregational tradition was certainly represented in the great Edinburgh Missionary Conference of 1910, which started the process that eventually led to greater cooperation not only in the mission field but also across the denominations generally. It was one of the first steps in what was to become the Ecumenical Movement. This gathered momentum after the First World War, during which the Forces' chaplains were prominent in addressing the frustrations of being inhibited in their ministry to the wounded and dying because of denominational rules.

The first Federal Council of Free Churches was established in 1919 and wider discussions with, among others, the Church of England soon followed. Such initiatives hastened the movement that led to the formation of the British Council of Churches in 1942. It is significant to note the date, which was of course during the Second World War. A Congregational Church in Worthing, learning of the plight of so many German people in the aftermath of the war, began to send parcels to a church in the Rhineland-Palatinate, beginning a friendship which still remains. The story is told in the book *Together Met, Together Bound* by the Rev. John

Reardon.[7] It is mentioned as just one example of what was later to become Inter-Church Aid, which itself was to grow into Christian Aid.

During the 1960s, when discussions between the Congregational and Presbyterian Churches pointed to the formation of the new denomination that became the United Reformed Church, a substantial number of Congregational Churches remained independent, within the overall guidance of the Congregational Federation. Some found it difficult to reconcile their independence with the security that belonging to a larger organisation would offer; for others the loss of their local autonomy to a conciliar structure was more important. There still remains the right of free thought and expression, which could lead to a very loose kind of composition. In fact, the system works because those who belong to it accept the principles, and share in their fellowship these common convictions of accepting the leadership found in the presence of Christ.

---

[7] John Reardon, *Together Met, Together Bound*, London, United Reformed Church, 2007

The Congregational Church in Bedford

The founding of the Howard Congregational Church in Mill Street arose out of a dispute with the then minister of the Bunyan Meeting, Joshua Symonds, who held office from 1766 to 1788. The well-known history of the church by H G Tibbutt[8] records how in February 1772 the Minister made a statement 'that he had adopted Baptist sentiments', after which he underwent his own baptism by immersion. This divided the Church, in a way that the Rev. Douglas Smith, minister of the Howard Church from 1938 to 1959, described in his foreword to Tibbutt's history as 'dissent from Dissent'. The prison reformer John Howard was among those who initiated the move, and his contributions led the subscription list started in April 1773. He later gave a further £200 towards the new building where worship began in 1775 with the first pastor Thomas Smith.

Thomas Smith left in 1796 and was succeeded by Thomas Burkitt. At this time it is recorded that there was 'a close relation-ship' between the three Mill Street churches (the third one being the Baptist church, which stood closer to the High Street, where the premises of the Royal Bank of Scotland currently stand). This relationship helped the newly formed Bedfordshire Union of Christians to flourish from 1797. The Howard church grew and continued to thrive so that by 1849 it had to be extended, with schoolrooms added for the Sunday school work in 1862: there were over 250 children to accommodate! The Literary Association was a notable feature of church life. A number of those who passed through the Church went on to distinguished careers in university life or to serve in the mission fields abroad. The church was represented on the Market Square when Gilbert's statue of John Howard was unveiled in 1894. One notable landmark was

---

[8] H G Tibbutt, *A History of Howard Congregational Church, Bedford*, published by the Church, 1961

the installation of electric lighting in 1897, the first church in Bedford to have done so.

The Howard Congregational Church continued to make a significant contribution to the town and community through the twentieth century. During the pastorate of the Rev. Victor Barradale (1908–1925), the congregation continued to increase, and weeknight activities included both Senior and Junior Bands of Hope, Christian Endeavour and the Mutual Improvement Society, which gave encouragement to many, not least the choir. They always met for practice on Friday evening, to lead the Sunday services and to give public performances of music. On Good Friday each year either Stainer's 'Crucifixion' or Maunder's 'Olivet to Calvary' would be performed at the little thatched Congregational church in the village of Roxton, and at Christmastime they would 'Come a Carolling'.

The Riverside Tennis Club was founded by Howard members during these years.

As the Second World War drew near, the ministry of Douglas Smith began, which was the high point of the church's life. After the war, the buildings were renovated, with a number of memorial windows being added to the one by Frank Salisbury, which marked the centenary of Howard's death in 1890. Activities added in these years included the Youth Club, the Men's Forum and the Girls' Life Brigade. For a short while there was also a Boys' Brigade. The women were well catered for, with an afternoon Guild and an evening Fellowship, together with a social programme in the Thursday Circle; these members met monthly to enjoy talks and outings.

When the Howard congregation joined St Luke's in a special service on Palm Sunday in 1971, they brought with them a tradition much wider than just Sunday worship. Their history embraced mission outreach, both at home and overseas, among children and young people, involvement in community work and a deep sense of fellowship with each other. This found obvious echoes in the Moravian traditions, already so important a part of St Luke's ethos. In fact, the union of the Moravian Church with the Congregational Church had been urged in an article in *The Messenger* of September 1939. In its widest interpretation, mission has always concerned the Congregational Church, which had supported the London Missionary Society, later to become the Council for World Mission. Various minute books record the many activities of members to raise the necessary funds from 1928 onwards.

One source of income was the collection of ship-ha'pennies by the children for the good ship *John Williams*. As a young missionary from Tottenham, John Williams sailed to Fiji in the early years of the nineteenth century and spent eighteen years working in the Pacific Islands. He returned to this country to raise money for a training college for pastors, retaining the ship (the *Camden*) for his use. When later he visited the New Hebrides in 1839 he was killed by cannibals. A new ship bearing his name was built in 1844 to carry on his work bringing hope and healing to many as well as the good news of the Gospel. Several successive ships bore the name, and the last of these, the *John Williams VII*, was named by HRH The Princess Margaret in August 1948, built at a cost of thirty-eight million ship ha'pennies. Home and overseas appeals worked in parallel until they combined in 1967.

The move to St Luke's and then into the United Reformed Church caused some confusion among these various committees, especially after the URC sought to bring all such efforts into a so-called Unified Appeal. The old missionary collecting boxes, some representing a thatched mud hut, are still treasured possessions. Other efforts, such as special missionary weekends, sales and stalls, coffee mornings and strawberry teas, talks and debates, musical evenings and garden parties, continued right up until 2005, when the Social Committee finally decided to call it a day.

There had been much encouragement for and from the village churches at this time, not only at Roxton but also with the Union Chapel at Cardington, opened in 1839 in what was known as the Old Barn. It also flourished, both among adults and children, and a new chapel was built in 1908 on land provided by Mr Samuel Whitbread, and subsequently known as the Howard Memorial Church. The relationship with the Howard Church remained and continued with St Luke's. Only a month after the closure of the Bedford Church Cardington celebrated the centenary of its building with a programme of events, culminating in the special service on 2 November 2008, at which the preacher was the Rev. John Proctor; he was director of New Testament Studies at Westminster College Cambridge and well known as a writer, particularly on St Matthew's Gospel. Among the former ministers to have accepted invitations to preach during these celebrations were the Rev. David Tatem and the Rev. Howard Starr.

The Rev. Douglas Smith's ministry at the Howard Church ended in 1959 with his appointment as one of the executive secretaries of the Congregational Union of England and Wales at their London headquarters. He was succeeded by the last minister at the Mill Street chapel, the Rev. Howard Starr, who also served as secretary to the Bedfordshire Congregational Union from 1966–68. When he moved on to the Wirral in 1970, he was not replaced. The approaching formation of the United Reformed Church led the denominational authorities to support the retention of only one place of worship in Bedford for this tradition of churchmanship, and the premises at St Luke's became that church in 1972.

Members of the Bedford Society appealed for the Howard building to be listed shortly before closure, and this was granted (Grade II). The church authorities announced their intention to redevelop the site, claiming that, as a church in use for worship, it had exemption from planning laws (the so-called ecclesiastical exemption of 1913). A difference arose as to the validity of this claim and this was tested in the courts. In 1973 the High Court ruled that Listed Building Consent was needed; in 1974 this was reversed in the Court of Appeal. The county council took the case to the House of Lords, which ruled that exemption applied only to alterations, and that Listed Building Consent was required for demolition. The church authorities waited for years before applying for permission to demolish and redevelop, and this was refused.

A public enquiry was held in 1983 and the decision was that redevelopment could take place, provided the 1849 façade was retained. Before anything was started, the buildings were badly damaged by fire in an act of vandalism on the eve of St Valentine's Day in 1985. The scarred ruins were left for many years until the site could be sold and developed. The façade was preserved, but according to the renovated plan of 1948, not of the original chapel. Its subsequent history as part of Bedford's leisure industry is hardly worthy of its previous standing in the town and a sad reflection indeed on society's standards today.

The bicentenary of the death of John Howard was acknowledged in two services at St Luke's in 1990. The first one was on Sunday, 21 January, bringing together as guests a number of distinguished visitors including the high sheriff, the deputy mayor and the chief constable, with Frances Crook, Director of the Howard League for Penal Reform and members of the prison and probation services. In his sermon, the Rt Rev. David Farmborough, the then-Bishop of Bedford, reflected on Howard's life of Christian service, travelling thousands of miles in order to make authorities aware of the appalling conditions in which prisoners were held. The Rev. Douglas Smith returned to offer prayers of intercession. Three weeks later a second service was held, this time the preacher being the Rt Rev. Trevor Huddleston who was, of course, associated with Bedford. It was a memorable day indeed, the very day on which news came of the forthcoming release of Nelson Mandela from prison in South Africa.

The tradition continues in Bedford at the Bunyan Meeting, which describes itself as 'Baptist and Congregational'. The relationship between this church and St Luke's has been cordial, and preachers have exchanged pulpits on many occasions. A number of members transferred there after closure. The Bunyan Meeting is a member of the Congregational Federation, and their current minister, the Rev. Christopher Damp, has served as the Federation's president. The church enjoys 'observer status' with the United Reformed Church, a rather vague situation which suggests there is at least a relationship.

The coming to St Luke's of the Howard congregation was acknowledged in the third of the presentations before the closure. Speaking on 'What it means to be Congregational', the Rev. Dr Stephen Orchard spoke of the long history within the tradition of the complete autonomy of the local congregation; from the outset the church had eschewed any form of centralised regulation. This dated back to Robert Brown in the latter part of the sixteenth century, and the first stirrings of the concept of the 'gathered' Church, which was not credal (as were the Presbyterians) but based on a covenantal understanding. The cry of the Separatists had been 'Come ye out from among them'. In those days the Church was seen as having a role to play for the State in keeping order among the people (a long way from the modern idea that in politics 'We don't do God'). Robert Brown saw the Church as being responsible only to God.

Dr Orchard traced the course of the restrictions cumulatively placed on Dissenters over the years, and reflected on how, during the eighteenth century, these were gradually dismantled. The founding of the County Unions in the nineteenth century arose from the desire to seek mutual support, and in parallel with the Roman Catholic Church, which was also finding its feet again, the Congregational Church became more assertive. All Churches in western culture are caught between ideas of local autonomy and the central structures that maintain orthodoxy. This, Dr Orchard said, would be a growing concern.

The Reformed Heritage

As has been noted already, there has long been a close association between the Congregational and Presbyterian churches; talks seeking closer cooperation nationally had begun as early as 1932. One report quotes the adage that 'they would not do separately what they could better do together', which reappeared later in ecumenical circles. The closing of the Howard Congregational Church and the fact that their minister was not replaced led to the expectation that only one of the churches in the tradition would survive to become the United Reformed Church in Bedford. One view shared with the writer suggested that the then-minister, the Rev. Harold Springbett, was anxious to complete arrangements for St Luke's to be that representative church in Bedford for the new structure before he retired. The move was welcomed by most people, and gradually the congregation became united despite the different backgrounds and expectations.

The new United Reformed Church officially came into being on 5 October 1972. (A point to note is that this move reintroduced the word 'Reformed' into the language of ecumenism.) A special Assembly was held during the morning in Westminster Central Hall in London to deal with the necessary enabling resolutions, and a service of worship followed in Westminster Abbey. The Archbishop of Canterbury, the Most Rev. Dr Michael Ramsey, and the Archbishop of Westminster, His Eminence Cardinal Heenan, were both present and took part. The ecumenical credentials of the new Church were thus established at the very beginning. Observers from the Reformed Church of Christ were present, which subsequently joined the new Church in 1981. Having started in the City of Westminster, events in the evening moved to the City of London: in the City Temple in Holborn, a less formal celebration was held for younger people, with pop music, dancing in the aisles to the music of *Godspell* and contributions from Donald Swann.

Writing in preparation for the Silver Jubilee of the United Reformed Church in October 1997, the then-interim moderator at St Luke's, the Rev. Roy Martin, remembered the original vision that underlay its creation:

> The United Reformed Church declares its intention, in fellowship with all the Churches, to pray and work for such visible unity of the whole Church, as Christ wills and in the way He wills...

These words form part of the basic Statement of the Nature, Faith and Order of the United Reformed Church, and the way in which the community of St Luke's had come together over the years gave substance to this hope.

Progress for St Luke's Church in its new identity was not easy. During this time, there were a number of significant initiatives of social outreach, but it all cost money. The situation which led to the closure in 2008 almost happened a decade earlier, when the need to update the facilities merely in order to sustain their work, let alone expand it, became clear. The *Bedford Herald* of 13 March 1997 reported that the church needed £360,000 to avoid closure then. Work with people with learning difficulties and for the Alzheimer's Support Group (known delightfully as 'Carers' Rest') had to be suspended pending improvements that were found to be necessary to the kitchens and toilets in order to comply with contemporary health and safety and hygiene regulations.

The appointment of the Rev. David Tatem in 1997 (he was inducted on 27 November) after a lengthy interregnum brought the necessary leadership, and under his guidance preliminary work began soon after the turn of the year. Funds were at last made available from the sale of the site of the old Howard Church in Mill Street, which had finally been accomplished; other grants were received from various local sources, helped by emphasising improvements for disabled access. This enabled the church to achieve the much-needed improvements to the buildings which were extensively used from the outset. Publicity at the time drew attention to the extent of the modern facilities available behind the otherwise rather drab exterior.

A company of the Girls' Brigade, originally from Howard,

continued as part of the life of the church, with a membership of about thirty; their banner hung in the church right to the end. A parallel company of the Boys' Brigade, although based at Priory Methodist Church, still met occasionally on the premises. A small congregation of Latvian Christians began to use the church for worship once a month under the care of the Very Rev. Juris Jurgis, Dean of the Latvian Evangelical Lutheran Church in Great Britain, based in Leicester.

Some consideration was given at this time to the idea of changing the usage of the buildings altogether. In 1989, the church elders initiated a feasibility study to identify areas in which the church might concentrate its resources, not least in reaching out to disadvantaged groups within the community. The Rev. Fred Linyard and the then-moderator of the Thames North Synod of the United Reformed Church, the Rev. Janet Sowerbutts, were both invited to lead discussions on the future (Janet was the first woman to be appointed a synod moderator in the new church structure.)

A community church committee was set up in 1993 which sought advice from an architect, Mr Terry Dacombe, on what work would be required to make possible such outreach. One suggestion was to adapt the whole suite of premises to provide a conference and retreats centre, but this was never pursued. It can be remarkably quiet in the burial ground behind the church, despite its proximity to the town centre; it would have made a splendid quiet garden. The societies working with those with learning difficulties and the Alzheimer's Support were both originally attracted to St Luke's because of the garden.

The proposals centred round ideas of implementing the work of the church in practical ways, as well as offering Christian fellowship and community work during the week. Another idea mooted at the time was for the community of St Luke's to move out of town and seek to develop a new church in an area scheduled for development. Elstow seemed a possibility, especially as the Bunyan Meeting owned a building there. Thoughts of cooperating with them in a joint initiative were expressed, but again it remained an idea that was never really explored. Hopes for attracting support from younger people, from the twenty-five- to forty-five-year-old group and for a clearer definition of the relationship between the URC as users and the Moravian Church as owners (a twenty-five-year agreement for security of tenure in return for improvements) were all mooted. As subsequent history has shown, not all of this was achieved, mainly through lack of funding but also because of the gradual decline of support, despite these very worthy intentions.

The new John Howard Hall – named appropriately after the prison reformer, as it was money from his church that had made it possible – was dedicated at a special service on 25 June 1998. The Rev. Janet Sowerbutts preached and readings from the Bible were given by Terry Dacombe, and by the Rev. John McOwat on behalf of the Moravian Church. Among those who subsequently made use of the hall were the Scottish and Welsh Societies of Bedford, reflecting their mainly Presbyterian allegiance.

The new facilities enabled the work with those adults in the community with mental handicap to be resumed, and under the leadership of the Rev. Derek Fitch and his wife, the idea of Cloisters was formed. Marion Swift and Kathleen Fitch, both teachers with experience of working with mentally handicapped children, visited a scheme already under way in Milton Keynes, and the visit bore fruit. Their impressive banner hung in the church on the north-west wall.

Provision was made for a group of twenty (no greater), who could develop a sense of social responsibility, as well as being encouraged to take part in worship that they could understand and to which they might contribute. The group would have its own funding drawn from ecumenical sources, and their meetings would allow them time to get to know each other through group support, conducted in their own but meaningful way. The Christian message was taught through music and story, activity and drama: the making of friezes was popular, as was the creation of an Easter garden. One activity that gave great pleasure was the ringing of handbells – not easy at the best of times. The achievements of each session would then be recorded in a book, and lead into lunch, which other members of the church might share. What was also shared was the pain and concern, for such a group would have all kinds of worries. A real sense of fellowship grew, as well as trust, and relationships deepened; two members were married in the church and spent some very happy years together.

The happy atmosphere was certainly noted when guests were entertained and among those giving encouragement was the Rev. Virginia Derr from the Pilgrim Church in New Bedford, USA. She was particularly impressed with her reception by the members of Cloisters. A link between St Luke's and Pilgrim, under the guidance of Kathleen Fitch, was maintained for about five years from 1985, and some members of St Luke's were able to visit.

Another initiative was taken by the Rev. David Tatem, who had been inducted to the pastorate at St Luke's in November 1997. This was on the Saturday before refurbishment work started on the Monday. Much of the motivation for the work had arisen from the fact that various activities had developed and were being carried out in the existing halls and garden, but with better facilities more could be done; the Alzheimer's Carers' group, for example, could meet inside and leave their charges safely in the enclosed garden area. Coupled with this was the realisation that the location of the church was not ideal for attracting new members. The question then was how to give the church a distinctive identity which would fill an important niche in the wider ecumenical scene in the town centre.

The answer almost presented itself. With the new halls and kitchen, St Luke's had by far the best suite of premises of any of the remaining town-centre churches, and was developing an ethos and a theology of service to the local community in affirming the worth of people as children of God. In February 1998, Mr Tatem contacted the director of social services at Bedfordshire County Council, Alan Chapman, to offer use of all the new facilities. His idea was to create a 'Community Church'. In subsequent conversations the idea of a cybercafé was mooted, in which the joys of modern computer technology could be opened up to people with learning disabilities. Access would be provided to such people to give them support, help and infor-mation in a sympathetic and supportive environment.

Two projects were envisaged, running in parallel, to offer those involved a range of opportunities for greater social inclusion through the use of computers, alongside training in catering skills. Financial support was gained from the Harpur Trust to obtain the furnishings and equipment needed. Staff from the Bedford Centre and from the council's environmental health and IT departments were involved, as were elders of the Church. The Barnfield College Adult Education Programme brought Jean Tunstall into the scheme to prepare the catering element of the café. Mr Tatem wrote of his lasting memory of when the first group of adults with learning difficulties paid their first visit to the kitchen in which they were to be taught how to cook.

> One of them with a look of wonder gazed around him and declared loudly that, 'It's beautiful!' Indeed it was, but it was also beautiful to recognise that they could experience something of the deliberate affirmation that they fully deserved the best and not the shoddy surroundings they had previously been expected to make do with.

The cybercafé was formally opened on 10 November 1999. More than a hundred people came to see the new computers and the artwork that arose from the Arthouse project running alongside it. To begin with, it was only open on Tuesdays and Wednesdays from 10.30 a.m. to 2.30 p.m. It was hoped to open up access to the Internet for the participants, and to link up with other day centres locally and more widely. Social Services, Learning Disability Services and Bedfordshire Advocacy Alliance were all involved. The clever title of this initiative combining computers and catering was Byte to Bite.

An important initiative taken by the people of St Luke's during the ministry of the Rev. Derek Fitch was to lead to the formation of BECHAR – the Bedford Concern for the Homeless and Rootless. The idea began with an appeal from the Cyrenians (based in Alexander Road) to the Bedford Council of Churches for help when they found themselves in financial difficulties, and Mr Fitch formed a committee to sort out the problem. Entry to those premises was by common consent of those already within, and this could lead to a degree of unfairness. Many were turned away to sleep rough.

A public meeting called at St Luke's drew around sixty or

seventy people and a steering committee was formed. The Anglican Sisters in Conduit Road gave lunches to the homeless, and there was a soup run in the evenings, but there was no provision for breakfast after a cold night on the streets. This gave St Luke's an opportunity, and for some time between twenty and thirty cooked breakfasts were served each day in the vestibule. This could only be a temporary measure, of course, and yet it took some six years of effort before sufficient funds were raised to buy the premises which BECHAR now operate in Prebend Street. The local council helped with a grant of £100,000.

Mr Fitch continued to serve as chairman of its directors until he reached the age of seventy. He tried to make it an ecumenical centre, but the Council of Churches would not take on the responsibility. Individually there were some very good and devoted helpers who cooked the meals and provided the essential focus for discussing problems. This stopgap process did achieve much until a more permanent arrangement could be made. BECHAR has been run as a charitable company since 1993, seeking to take 'a holistic approach to helping people take the next step towards reintegration into the community'.

Until 2005, the St Luke's premises were still used over Christmas to provide lunches and access to advice and some treatments for the homeless community – estimated over Christmas 2008 still to number some 200 people. Changes in personnel and improvements to the facilities at the Prebend Street premises led to the decision to keep the provision in-house from 2006. The charity has a wide brief, offering shelter and food, tea and coffee, facilities for personal hygiene, access to health care and, where appropriate, counselling. Questions of drug and alcohol dependence can also be addressed, and advice for claiming benefits is offered. It provides a very valuable service with the one aim of improving the quality of life for those who need it most, and St Luke's can be proud of having instigated it.

One dimension of the initiative that did not quite develop as had been hoped was the setting up of one office as a 'hot-desk room' for small charities trying to get started. Under the scheme they were encouraged to rent the room, fitted as it was with telephone access and computer facilities, for set times of the week until they got established. In fact, two rooms were so provided, but each found a worthy tenant.

One was what came to be known as BRASS – Bedfordshire Refugee and Asylum Seeker Support. This began in 1999, using office space in the Minister's House, and developed into a scheme offering help and support to some of the most vulnerable members of the town community. The quality of the service was acknowledged by gaining the approval of the Office of the Immigration Services Commissioner. It was difficult work, for the people that BRASS sought to help were not the most popular. Some of them had been detained in the Yarl's Wood Immigration Detention Centre just to the north of the town, and others faced deportation, or questions about the legality of their status. Publicity was sought through exhibitions during Refugee Week each year, which was sometimes the target of unsympathetic attention. The director, Mr Bryden Keenan, gained recognition for his work in civic awards for his service to these people.

The other room was used by the Langley House Trust for their work in support of ex-offenders. It was conveniently close to the prison and to other legal offices and probation services in the town centre. This work was also deeply appreciated by many of the vulnerable members of the community. The trust celebrated its fiftieth anniversary during 2008, and the writer and two other members of the eldership of the church were invited as guests to the celebration reception held in the House of Lords in October at which the speaker was HRH The Princess Royal.

Since 1987 each act of worship at St Luke's has begun with the lighting of the Peace Candle and a prayer for peace. This, too, has an interesting history. It was in May 1986 that an American Presbyterian minister from York, Pennsylvania, visited Russia with a group of American Christians. At a service in an Orthodox church, an old woman pressed a note into his hand and asked him to use the money (which she could ill afford) to buy a candle and to light it at every service in his church as a symbol of peace. The minister was deeply touched by this gesture, and on his return he bought a candle in a small glass, and with the full support of his church kept it on the communion table and indeed lit it at every service, as the old woman had requested.

The idea spread and more candles were purchased and sent to other churches with the same request that they should prompt prayers for peace. Two of the minister's congregation had been members of a URC congregation in the West Midlands, and they sent a candle to their old church asking them to take up the chain of prayer. This they did, and it quickly spread in this country, too. One of the members of St Luke's came from that church and introduced the idea here. The candle was first lit on Advent Sunday, 29 November 1987. More candles were purchased and sent off to contacts in other places so that the peace prayer itself spreads ever more widely. It is an example of a simple gesture on the part of a poor old woman that has grown far beyond what she could ever have imagined. Through her simple gesture so many people are using the focus of the little candle for a universal and regular prayer for peace throughout the world.

Over these years the community of St Luke's made a significant contribution to the life of the wider Church in ministerial training. An American student minister, the Rev. Carrie Brain, spent a period at St Luke's in training under the leadership of Mr Fitch. She spent a great deal of her time and energies working with the younger generation which is fondly remembered by many of them. During Mr Springbett's time as minister, the Rev. Cecil White candidated for the ministry of the United Reformed Church and trained at Westminster College, Cambridge. He was ordained in 1987 and served first at Hove in Sussex. He then moved to Darnall in Sheffield, which was in ecumenical partnership with its Anglican neighbours. This began a sequence of neat coincidences. The parish priest at Darnall was the Rev. Mike Fudger, who later moved to be the new incumbent at St Peter de Merton in Bedford. The writer was a colleague of Cecil's during his period of time in Sudbury in Suffolk, and after his move to St Luke's, Cecil's wife, also a URC minister, moved to the writer's former pastorate.

The Rev. John Wilkinson also spent time at St Luke's serving an internship year with the Rev. Derek Fitch, and lived with his wife in the Sisters' House. He too is remembered for his work among the younger community at the Church. He was also a student at Westminster College, and was ordained in 1990 to serve in Northwich before a later move to Oxford. The Rev. Keith Brown, a former teacher and accomplished musician, also candidated during Mr Fitch's ministry; for a while he had been organist at St Luke's and did valuable work with the choir. After training at Westminster, he was ordained in 1992 and served in Luton for a number of years before retiring locally.

The Rev. Yolande Burns served her internship year under Mr Tatem, arriving at St Luke's as a mature student in 1999. From her home in Buckden she gave valuable support to the whole range of church life at St Luke's and was much loved. She was very involved with Cloisters, and is remembered for her astute conduct of all-age worship. She was also engaged with the Open Book project, which took Bible stories into local schools.

As if this were not enough, she used her musical gifts at Christmas in 1999 to produce Garth Hewitt's Christian Aid musical *The Feast of Life*, bringing together talents from St Luke's, from the Howard Church at Cardington and members of the Girls' Brigade. The members of Cloisters began with carols played on the hand bells. The performance incorporated songs, narratives and projected images to engage the audience in thinking about the work of Christian Aid, and ended with the distribution of Christingles to embrace the Moravian tradition. She also studied at Westminster, and the college acknowledged that her time at St Luke's had been particularly successful; the work of the support group had been especially pleasing. After her ordination in 2001, she ministered first in Wisbech and Long Sutton before moving to Lancaster North in 2006; her pastorate there involves a chaplaincy with the RAF.

As well as these ordained ministers St Luke's has contributed to the training of lay preachers, among them Bill Fortescue, an elder and former church treasurer. The writer has also been a tutor for the United Reformed Church's Training for Learning and Serving scheme, which oversees the training of students for preaching and other areas of service in the life of our churches.

The links between St Luke's Church and Westminster College, Cambridge have long been recognised in many ways. When the writer was inducted to the pastorate of St Luke's on 27 November 2004, he was presented by the Rev. Dr Janet

Tollington, who had been interim moderator during the vacancy. Music was given a prominent place in the service. The moderator of the Thames North Synod at the time, the Rev. Roberta Rominger and the writer performed an aria from Bach's Magnificat in D major, BWV 243, 'Quia fecit mihi magna' which has a cello obbligato; Joanna Martin played the organ continuo.

Music also featured in a service that illustrated the warmth of fellowship at St Luke's, and that again emphasised the close cooperation between St Luke's and the parish Church of St Peter de Merton. Under the leadership of their then-director of music, Graham Hyden, a gathered choir would meet once a month to sing a full choral evensong, and this robed choir was engaged for a service on 18 April 2006 to mark the twenty-fifth anniversary of the writer's ordination. The service began with Anton Bruckner's motet 'Locus iste' and included Stanford's magnificent setting of the Magnificat in C. The anthem was the 'Hallelujah' chorus from *Messiah*, which the choir had rehearsed for Easter. The preacher at this service was the Rev. Elizabeth Caswell, who had been the writer's moderator in the Eastern Synod (the setting of his previous pastorate) in her role as moderator-elect of the General Assembly of the United Reformed Church; she had been instrumental in arranging the writer's move to Bedford. She pointed to a feature of the service that she thought was unique: that the writer had been ordained on his birthday. As it was a birthday, the celebratory buffet in the hall afterwards included jelly and ice cream!

One element that encouraged the formation of the new church was the coming together in 1970 of two important bodies: one was the World Alliance of Reformed and Presbyterian Churches and the other the International Congregational Council. It would be wrong to attribute a single definition to the idea of being Reformed, for this is an elusive concept. The Rev. Dr Janet Tollington explored this in her presentation, the last of the four in the sequence. The Reformed Churches in the various European nations can all trace their origins back to Luther, Calvin and Zwingli, and yet there are distinct differences in the traditions of the Dutch, Hungarian and Swiss Churches. The word was reintroduced into this country in 1972, but even so it has changed since its inception. The different ways of transcribing the word is significant – is it 'Reformed' or 're-formed'? *Semper reformanda*. The experience and example of history shows that there is a gap between Church and state; when the two sides make conflicting demands, it is the example of Christ that must be upheld first, a point which the Statement of the Nature Faith and Order of the United Reformed Church still maintains.

There is diversity in unity which is of lesser importance if the focus is on Christ – even Calvin knew this. The commitment to ecumenism flows from the Reformed identity; each part must acknowledge the other parts if it is to create effective witness to God's love for the world. The Reformed tradition is not defined in one set of ideas. It brings together scripture, worship and ministry in a way that has few certainties but which is open to change as impelled by Christ to address the needs of a world that is constantly changing.

A very important point is that for the Reformed Church the Trinitarian view of God is vital. The Church reflects the body of Christ which is the community of the Spirit under God; this is why it was called into being and what it represents. The Reformed community maintains the belief in the absolute centrality of the scriptures and of the Word of God: are they the same thing? Some adhere strictly to the doctrine of the infallibility of scripture; others accept a relative view which is open to revelation. It is more important not to lose sight of the corporate identity of the Church. The Bible is the story of God's people, the document through which God's purposes of love are revealed, especially in Jesus. Yet the risen Jesus is now the living Word of God, who continually guides us by the Spirit to understand the Bible. This underlines the importance of biblical literacy. The first booklet in the United Reformed Church's Vision4Life series is 'Transformed by the Bible', pointing to a greater significance and awareness of scripture; thus the Church should discern the voice of God above the clamour of the world, and see the mission of God in Christ that is going on without us.

Then there is the centrality of grace expressed in the Gospels, the work of reconciliation through Christ's actions and not through our own merit. This is the truth we are called upon to proclaim, and to be free to live as God's children in God's world. It is not an easy task, but grace enables us to believe in the goodness of God and to express it in the way we live. The Gospel calls us to receive the sacraments within the Church, to offer worship which is passionate and meaningful, enabling us to express community. This is done not least through evangelism, which is not just the task of the minister but central to the core idea of the priesthood of all believers. God empowers all to engage in this work, which has important implications for our future.

The Organ

Music has played a very important part in the life of St Luke's United Church from the very beginning. It was resolved as early as June 1747 'to have a Musick Gallery built at the End of the Chapel over against the Other Gallery & the Musicians Are to Keep their Instruments there and Exercise'. The standard was not always adequate, for it was recorded soon afterwards that 'it was thought best to drop our Musick o' Sundays for the Present … and the Musick Matters will be thought of & regulated'.

The organ has contributed greatly to the history of the church and its worship. As was noted earlier, the old instrument used from the mid-1830s was originally built for the parish Church of St Paul in Bedford. It came from the workshop of Gerhardt Schmidt, nephew of the great eighteenth century organ builder Father Bernard Schmidt, who installed instruments in St Paul's Cathedral and in the Temple Church. The cost was met by public subscription, and donations were notably received from the Earls of Elgin, Aylesbury and Ashburnham, together with over a hundred other members of the nobility.

The first organist to use it at St Paul's was William Weale (1670?–1727) who composed the tune 'Bedford'; the bells in the tower played the tune in carillon style for over a century. The original carved oak case that was created for the organ included cherubic heads; the angel with the trumpet was added in 1736. The instrument was extended by Hancock and Craig in 1782, and again by William Allen of London in 1802. By 1832 it had fallen into disrepair, bearing, according to one report, 'traces of having been very much ill-used at some period of its history' and on the advice of an organ builder was replaced with a bigger and better one. This old organ was kept in what was described as 'some obscure part of the belfry' until it was sold to the Moravians for £50.

In its new setting the organ was originally installed in the

Source unknown, from church records

choir gallery of the Moravian Church. The work was started by Henry Cephas of Lincoln, but when he doubled the bill it was transferred to John Smith of Bristol. The gilt rising sun was added to the case at this point to hide the swell box. The trumpeting angel was once above it; it bears an inscription on a tablet behind the wings recording that it was 'The Gift of Mr Francis Walker, alderman, and Mr John Russell, common councillor, 1736.' Originally also of oak, it was at one stage found to be riddled with woodworm and repaired with fibreglass.

The original instrument had two manuals (great and swell) and pedals. Further enlargement was carried out by James Eagles in 1852 and 1858, which resulted in 'a mutilated and patched-up instrument' according to Wilfred Smith's 1945 history. For much of the time it was 'difficult to play, and nearly always out of order' (ibid). When the church was rebuilt in 1865 the organ was placed in a chamber on the west side; traces of the arch can still be distinguished in the plaster of the wall. The compass of the swell was extended and couplers added, and the remainder re-voiced. It was then further extended in 1876 'that it might be rendered capable of properly sustaining its important part in the services of the church'.

A third manual was added by James Trustram of Bedford. New stops were added from an unknown London source, by which time very little of the original 1715 instrument remained. One comment in the description of 1876 was to prove ironic in view of what was to happen in the 1970s: it was decided 'to exclude all appliances that belong more properly to concert-room instruments'. The opening recital on this new configuration was given by Frederic Archer, who was then the organist at the Alexandra Palace in London. The registration of that time is given at the end of this chapter.

Another move took place in 1888 when the apse was added to the north to accommodate the choir stalls. The case was extended to provide the sumptuous climax to the sanctuary. The work on the instrument was carried out by Brindley and Forster of Sheffield, who added tubular-pneumatic action, with additional bourdon stops on the pedals. This latest version was opened with great ceremony in July 1888. The mayor and corporation attended the morning service, there was a Lovefeast in the afternoon and Bishop Blandford from Malmesbury preached in the evening.

In August of that year, the Moravian Synod met in the newly appointed church. At regular intervals, further remedial work was found to be necessary, and a number of ingenious schemes were tried to provide sufficient air. For the first fifty years it was blown by hand, and suggestions were made for both gas and water power. In 1910 an electric blower was installed with variable wind pressure operated by a bicycle wheel. This lasted until 1944 when the supply of suitable bicycle tyres gave out because of the war. A new electric blower was installed in 1945 in preparation for the bicentenary celebrations, but by 1955 the instrument had become unplayable. The work now undertaken was done without professional advice or oversight, and the legacy thus left was embarrassing. The complex mechanism needed a very high wind pressure, which the system was not always able to supply. Two firms of organ restorers declared that it was uneconomic even to contemplate repairs. The Rev. Harold Springbett was told that it should simply be thrown on to a bonfire.

Source unknown, from church records

The assistant organist at the time, Mr Peter Lightfoot, saw this as a challenge. Under his enthusiastic leadership, extensive repairs were undertaken by members of the congregation over a number of years. An estimated 900 man-hours were devoted to installing some twelve miles of wire, to soldering 12,000 joints and electrifying the action. Enthusiasm, even sincere, can never match trained expertise, and the essential nature of the instrument was lost.

A number of elements were then obtained from cinema organs then being frequently dismantled, and used to try and expand the instrument. Some parts were taken from a Christie electronic organ that had once entertained cinema audiences in the Theatre Royal in Elephant and Castle. One unit chest may have come from the Astoria in Streatham; a number of stop-keys remained from the console, long since discarded, which were originally fitted into the Rivoli Cinema in Southend. Some Wurlitzer parts had been imported from the Fulton Theatre in Cleveland, Ohio, subsequently modified for the Metropole Cinema in London's Victoria. Two Wurlitzer switch stack actions came from the New Victoria cinema in Preston. Other parts came from the Conacher and Compton workshops, and a few parts from the respected firm of Hill, Norman & Beard. It was a strange, even eclectic, mixture; but then, even the Psalmist drew on a variety of sources to praise the Lord, and the organ as it stood in latter years could have reproduced all the sounds listed in Psalm 150!

A number of concerts were centred round the organ in its new format; it had three manuals and sixty-five stops. It was rededicated on 11 November 1978 at a service in memory of Peter Lightfoot, who had died without seeing the fulfilment of his dream. The choir of St Luke's was joined by those of the Bunyan Meeting and Christchurch, Hitchin. The music included the Widor 'Toccata', Stanford's magnificent 'Magnificat in C' and the 'Carillon Sortie' by Mulet. A concert in September 1980 included a number of instrumental solos, and the Rev. Keith Brown played Walton's 'Crown Imperial'. Indeed the use of the church for music was increasing, and a good reputation for performance was backed up by a considerable library of musical scores. In a way, it was the sheer weight of enthusiasm that brought about the downfall of the historic instrument. Despite the many hours of devoted attention, the organ needed more skilled oversight; tuning and voicing demand much more than mere enthusiasm. The organ expert John Norman, in his report on the instrument in 1997, described it as 'a surprising mixture of disparate elements … carried out in a rather haphazard manner'. In the circumstances, this is almost kind.

In 1998, the attempts to maintain the instrument were abandoned in favour of purchasing an Eminent model from Cathedral Organs of Welwyn, the speakers for which were installed behind the pipes of the screen. This gave the sound an air of verisimilitude, and it served the congregation well until the closure. The magnificent oak screen from the 1715 organ, complete with its angel, was then donated by the Moravian Church authorities to St Paul's, to be rebuilt as part of the improvements to the organ there. It is wonderful to think that it will still be accessible to the public in a place of worship in the centre of Bedford; indeed it will have returned home, and a significant part of St Luke's will have survived.

On the Friday afternoon before the closure, news was received from the Department of Culture, Media and Sport that the church, in consultation with English Heritage, had been listed at Grade II. This meant, of course, that nothing could be removed from the church without the permission of the Borough Council Planning Department after a suitable enquiry had been held. The Listing Notice specifically mentioned 'significant elements of an organ, built in 1715 by the noted organ builder Gerard Smith'. Meantime, interested officers of the Cinema Organ Society had been in touch, anxious to gain access to what survived of the electronic organ. Permission was gladly given, and a range of parts both great and small was removed to add to the resources available to the society. An official of the borough believed that this broke the terms and conditions of the listing, and the minister was even threatened with prosecution if this had been found to be the case. The material, it was said, might have to be brought back (from Ipswich) and reinstalled! It took a lot of work through additional letters, telephone calls and messages, backed up by further documentation faxed from officers of the society, before the local official was finally convinced that the 1960s remnants of redundant electronic cinema organs, gathered from cardboard boxes or even from the floor, had nothing to do with the historic pipe organ of old, which, apart from the screen, no longer existed. The writer appealed against the wording of the listing, on the grounds that it referred specifically to the 1715 instrument, which in fact was no longer extant. Insisting on the evidence of a report from officers of the British Institute of Organ Studies, the appeal was rejected, despite the fact that no elements of the 1715 organ exist, and nothing from the original instrument survives apart from the screen. Meanwhile, the Eminent instrument was returned to the workshop, serviced and eventually sold on for further use in the United Reformed Church in Stevenage.

The registration after the 1876 reconfiguration and improvements was as follows:

Great

Large open diapason 8'
Small open diapason 8'
Stopped diapason 8'
Principal 4'
Twelfth 3'
Fifteenth 2'
Sesquialtera 3 ranks
Trumpet 8'

Swell

Bourdon 16'
Open diapason 8'
Stopped diapason 8'
Keraulophon 8'
Principal 4'
Twelfth 3'
Fifteenth 2'
Mixture 2 ranks
Hautboy 8'
Cornupean 8'

Choir

Dulciana 8'
Stopped diapason 8'
Dulcet 4'
Flute 4'
Clarionet 8'
Piccolo 2'

Pedal

Open diapason 16'
Pedal octave coupler

Couplers

Swell to Great unison
Choir to Swell unison
Swell to Swell octave
Swell to Swell suboctave
Great to pedals
Swell to pedals
Choir to pedals
Six combination pedals

Total number of pipes: 1518

The Final Legacy

So much has been lost in the last fifty years, and society has changed. Minutes and church records of the 1950s regularly refer to there being more than 160 communicants at a communion service at St Luke's on a Sunday morning, and the premises were in constant use for a variety of activities by so many different age groups, both within and beyond the membership. After the turn of the millennium, the age profile of the members was increasing, and the style of worship and churchmanship, though appreciated by the members, seemed no longer to appeal to the wider Church community. In the four years of the writer's ministry no new members were admitted, no weddings were conducted and only three baptisms took place; but there were seven funerals, together with another twenty-five at the crematorium, including a number of those who had contributed greatly to the life of St Luke's.

The first warning of impending closure was defined in a letter to the Moravian and United Reformed Church leaders in January 2007. A number of factors coming together began to place an unsustainable burden on the available resources, both human and financial. Individually they might have been addressed, but cumulatively they proved to be insurmountable. The organist resigned for health reasons, and the strength of the eldership diminished because of infirmity or decisions to move elsewhere. Those remaining were beset by a number of underlying tensions, but no more than can be expected in such a community.

Certain points of focus proved to be an obstacle for some, the troublesome question of sexuality among them. The United Reformed Church sets out to be totally inclusive at all levels of its councils, and one pastoral situation arose in the congregation which the St Luke's community addressed with their usual tolerant acceptance and loving fellowship. At the annual Assembly of the United Reformed Church in 1999, it had become clear that this vexatious question over sexuality threatened to divide the

Church, and it was decided to put in place a seven-year moratorium on discussing it in public. It was hoped that during the intervening time a new and acceptable direction would emerge from wider consultation among the Churches, but this did not happen. The liberal understanding was not accepted by all the members of St Luke's. A few left, not wishing to be associated with the church at such a time.

The buildings in St Peter's Street were looking tired, and the means required to refurbish them were simply not available. For some time now, the Moravian membership had been so small as to be almost insignificant, making the United Reformed congregation almost into squatters. A proposed lease was drawn up to regularise the situation, but it was never ratified, as the terms demanded would have been impossible to meet when closure inevitably came. It was interesting to discover the following passage, written in 1964 and reflecting on the contribution to the life of the church made by the Presbyterian members:

> What did the future offer this congregation? Was it to be a slow fading till reality had to be faced, and as with many downtown congregations, the Church and Manse sold to become offices or a shop? Or was there hope that the Spirit might blow again and new life come?

As has been noted already, some serious questions about the future life of the church and certainly of its buildings had also been addressed in 1992. It was thought then that any such development must be undertaken ecumenically. It was said in the introduction to this history that the writer was called to Bedford to oversee precisely such a move, which did not work out. What followed the exploration of those fears in 1964 then enabled the church to function for another half-century.

That half-century was one of considerable achievement. Even in the early 1990s there was something going on at the church every day, with a comprehensive and varied programme addressing a wide range of tastes and activities. The main service on a Sunday morning was even then still attracting the support of about 120 regular worshippers. Certain questions now arose that for some were to prove challenging, but which brought out the best of Christian love and support from others. Attempts to move the focus of the church's outreach were not universally welcomed, not least because of the inherent demands on the resources of a declining and aging congregation. The use of neighbouring buildings in the street, especially in exploiting leisure opportunities, was beginning to attract the attention of large numbers of younger people, and the older members were less willing to come out in the evenings to attend events. Returning late one evening to the church premises, the writer had to pass through a long queue of potential customers to the adjacent nightclub premises, which stretched well beyond the gateway to St Luke's. Society was changing fast in its attitude to the Churches and the decline in numbers was swift. It is a reflection of changing tastes and attitudes that those Churches that now are flourishing seem to be those that are more determinative in regard to what is acceptable in terms of doctrine.

The catalyst that hastened the decision to close was the loss of a major hiring contract which had been using the premises for a training course as part of the programme of Barnfield College with the cybercafé initiative; by now this had petered out. The college governors decided to gather all such courses on a single site in Queen's Park, and they gave due notice; this meant the loss at a stroke of more than half the church's income. Administrative assistance had been hired for a time to oversee the increasing demands on the premises but this had to be withdrawn. Even without this, annual running costs for the church were about £25,000 but regular income was down to about £13,000. The costs involved in complying with the increasing demands of health and safety legislation and the Disability Discrimination Act had had an effect. The number of people regularly coming to worship and able to hold office had now dropped to about thirty.

Faced with the inevitable, the closure date of 5 October 2008 was chosen to give sufficient time for the requisite administration to be followed through and for which it was expected that sufficient funds could still be available. The vacancy caused by the move of the Rev. David Tatem to Milton Keynes in 2003 had lasted eighteen months, and soon after the writer's appointment the then-Rector of St Peter's, the Rev. Guy Buckler, moved to

Bushey. This meant a total of two-and-a-half years in which no progress could be made towards uniting the two congregations of St Luke's and St Peter's; and in that period both interest and momentum were lost. The town-centre location meant that the site of the church was no longer part of any definable residential community. Other Free Churches which had earlier moved out to the expanding estates to the north and east of the town were flourishing, with excellent modern facilities to meet modern expectations. The church community at St Peter's began to question their possible longer-term commitment to the work of the United Reformed and Moravian Churches with an increasingly elderly congregation; ecumenical agreement would have meant legally binding commitments that would have become irrelevant within a few years. New proposals from the Anglican Church under the heading of 'Ecumenical Hospitality' meant that a shared relationship with fewer regulations became possible. It is noteworthy that when the decision to close was made, no one abandoned membership; it was noted above that throughout the four years of the writer's ministry no new members were admitted. The core fellowship remained together until the final day of worship on Sunday, 5 October 2008.

It can be said with conviction that the demise of St Luke's was not due to the failure of its witness. Right to the end there was an obvious and genuine sense of commitment, which was reflected in the very real sense of holiness in worship. There was still a vibrant spiritual response in the services, and the encouraging and sympathetic support given to the sick and housebound was exemplary. Often the writer would learn of the circumstances of illness or distress, only to find that members of the congregation were already addressing the needs that had arisen. The visit of the Rt Rev. Beth Torkington, the first woman bishop of the British province of the Moravian Church, to take a service in June 2008, is remembered for her sensitive and meaningful message of encouragement.

For some time a sequence of silhouettes, cut from black sugar paper by Marion Swift, had adorned the windows behind the gallery. Throughout the final year, these reflected the milestones of the progress towards closure. The eastern one displayed representations of harvest and Christmas, the central one showed the Lamb and Flag of the Moravian Church with the date 1745, the founding of the Bedford Church; and the letters 'URC' with the fish and the cross and the date of 1984, when the agreement setting up St Luke's United Church was made. Between them, the sequence of Palm Sunday, Good Friday and Easter Day was shown. In the western window was the symbol of Pentecost and references to the hymns used in the final service, including 'Lord, for the years your hand has kept and guided'. In the roundels above were symbols of the bread and wine, the cross and the peace candle and the dove of peace. Pictures of these appeared more than once in *The Moravian Messenger*. This work was featured in an interview with the writer recorded by the *Times and Citizen*, film of which was made available on websites.

One remarkable fact highlighted the closing date for the writer. Mention has already been made to the annual publication since 1730 by the Moravian Church of a textbook and almanac, which offers a 'watchword' for every day of the year. Published in over fifty languages, it uses biblical texts and verses from hymnody as a focus for prayer and fellowship throughout the Moravian community and beyond. The binding of the writer's copy for the year 2008, though never ill-treated, broke in two: the break occurred at the page dated 5 October.

Before closure could happen, the Moravian Synod had to agree to it by way of a resolution. The Synod was held in July 2008 at the Hayes in Swanwick, and the bland and unemotional wording of Proposal 8 hid an anguished sadness. It was proposed by the writer and seconded by Sr Gwen Gribble:

Be it proposed that Synod:

1. Notes the Bedford St Luke's congregation will cease to meet for worship on Sunday, 5 October 2008;

2. Resolves to give up the work there with grateful thanks to all who have served and witnessed to Christ in the Bedford St Luke's and formerly St Peter's congregation for the past 263 years; and

3. Requests that Section 2:1 of the Book of Order under the list of recognised congregations – Eastern District – be amended by the deletion of Bedford St Luke's (Moravian/URC).

In her supporting submission, Sr Gribble quoted in her concluding remarks the words of a hymn by Joseph Hart (1712–68), who attributed his re-conversion to a sermon heard in the Fetter Lane Moravian Church in London in 1757, after which he became the minister of the Independent Chapel in Jewin Street:

> 'Tis Jesus the first and the last,
> Whose Spirit shall guide us safe home;
> We'll praise him for all that is past,
> And trust him for all that's to come.[9]

The resolution was carried, with expressions of support, sympathy and thanks.

A similar process was necessary in the councils of the United Reformed Church at their Synod in London held on 8 November 2008. The resolution before the Synod was as follows:

> Synod approves the closure of St Luke's United Church, Bedford, with effect from 5 October 2008.

The writer spoke of the reasons behind the closure, described in the subsequent minutes as 'detailed and thoughtful', and the moderator, the Rev. Dr Andrew Prasad, expressed appreciation of his ministry and of all those who had contributed to the worship life of St Luke's.

Following closure, a number of assets belonging to St Luke's found further use elsewhere. The copies of the Moravian Hymn Book were sent to a number of Moravian churches in the West Indies – an interesting link with the earliest days of mission! Copies of the URC hymnbook *Rejoice and Sing* were moved to the Bunyan Meeting and the pew Bibles, the New Revised Standard Version, found a new home at St Peter's to augment their own collection. Some of the kitchen equipment went to the Boys'

---

[9] Quoted from *Rejoice and Sing*

Brigade, still run by a former member of the church but now based at Priory Methodist Church. The upholstered chairs were much appreciated by the members of the congregation at St Mary's parish church in Goldington. Parts of the communion set eventually found their way to a church in Ghana. A number of items of interest were accepted by the Bedford Museum. After planned extensions to their premises, it is proposed that a display of the history of religion in the town should include these. The written records were deposited, along with older books from the constituent congregations, with the Bedfordshire and Luton Archives and Records Service. Some of the framed lists of names were given to Queen's Park Moravian and to the Howard Memorial Church at Cardington.

The final day of worship evoked very mixed emotions. The choir of twenty-four singers was drawn from those at St Peter's, St Paul's and St Mary's, Goldington, who had been meeting at St Peter's as a 'gathered' choir to sing a full choral evensong once a month. They had rehearsed the music on the Saturday afternoon under the direction of Mr Graham Hyden; he had recently moved away from the town but returned for the weekend. On the Sunday morning, sixty-five were present for the last communion, which was designed 'for the family of the Church'. Among them were a number of former ministers, including the Rev. Fred Linyard and the Rev. David Tatem. Hymns included Brian Wren's modern 'Great God, your love has called us here' and the poetic gem from the seventeenth century by John Mason, 'How shall I sing that majesty', reflecting back to its inclusion in the minister's service of induction in 2004.

Eighty guests then had lunch in the hall, supplied by caterers. Marion Swift had prepared an exhibition on the four denominations in parallel with the four presentations during the final month, which was displayed in the vestibule and later along the east wall of the church; it attracted considerable interest.

For the afternoon service, the church was full; over 200 people came from, among other places, Dorchester, Hereford and Edinburgh. The moderator of the General Assembly of the United Reformed Church, the Rev. John Marsh, gave a splendid address, profound but with light touches, encouraging and supportive – St Luke's has long enjoyed a reputation as a preaching church. He had chosen pilgrimage as the theme of his moderatorial year. The traditional symbol of Christian pilgrimage is the scallop shell, which is especially associated with the journey to the burial place of the apostle James at Santiago di Compostela in north-western Spain, a journey he himself had made. Everyone present at the General Assembly of the United Reformed Church that summer in Edinburgh had been given such a shell with the encouragement to continue their personal pilgrimage in fellowship with the whole church. The members of St Luke's were encouraged to take their scallop shells to their new place of worship, where they would be blessed as a mark of continuing fellowship. The one given to the minister came 'with the thanks of the United Reformed Church for his diligent and caring ministry, and as a sign and symbol of the holy pilgrimage we make together as God's People'.

Hymns at this final service included the great Moravian paean 'Christian hearts in love united', written by Count Nicholas von Zinzendorf himself in 1723, and finally 'God is working his purpose out as year succeeds to year'. The music group New Life from Cardington also took part, acknowledging the link with the Howard Congregational Church in St Luke's history.

The first part of the service was filmed by Anglia Television and used in that evening's local news and in further bulletins over the following twenty-four hours. Several messages of prayerful support were received from many Moravian colleagues, including both the bishops of the Unity, from Jackie Morten of the Provincial Board (who was in Tanzania at the time) and from Br Henning Schlimm on behalf of the Moravian European Bishops' Conference. The service has been acknowledged as a fine and glorious ending to the tradition of worship at St Luke's, which is exactly what was wanted. The new Synod moderator, the Rev. Dr Andrew Prasad, was there, having been inducted to office only the day before, and spoke briefly, and the Bishop of Bedford, the Rt Rev. Richard Inwood, spoke on behalf of the other Churches in his capacity as Chairman of Bedfordshire Ecumenical Committee. Continuing to the last the long tradition of music, the service began with S S Wesley's 'Lead me, Lord', the anthem was C Hubert Parry's 'I was glad' and the very last notes of music heard in the church came from the Moravian 'Hosanna' anthem. As that came to an end so did the service, with no postlude on the organ; the members of the congregation were left in silence, to move, or stay, or wonder, as they felt moved. It was a telling moment.

The Moravian Church had looked to its own future in 1998, and worked with the Church of England to draw up what became known as the Fetter Lane Agreement in 1998. This enabled the two Churches to acknowledge a greater degree of cooperation and acknowledgement. It seems, therefore, not inappropriate that the life of St Luke's would in a small way continue in association with one of Bedford's oldest Anglican Churches, that of St Peter de Merton. In a commemorative service in Manchester Cathedral celebrating the tenth anniversary of the Fetter Lane Agreement, the words of one of the great figures of Moravian history were quoted. In 1660, John Amos Comenius commended the care of his beloved Moravian Church to the Church of England:

> To you, our friends, we commit, according to the example of the same Divine Master, that which is far better, our dear mother our Church herself. Take up the care of her now in our stead, because in her life she has gone before you for over two centuries, with examples of faith and patience.

These words have found a new resonance in the present and they speak to us afresh.

The sale of the property to Bedford School was completed soon after that date. This, too, would have pleased Comenius, who was known by many as the father of modern education. The school authorities plan to absorb the buildings into the life of the school, perhaps using some of them as a space for performance in the next stage of their development plan, which they are not quite ready to implement at this time. Their assurance to respect the history and integrity of the building was a gesture deeply appreciated by all the members of the church and by the denominational authorities.

The definition of a United Reformed Church is one that is governed by its church meeting, and the final one was held on

31 March 2009 in the parish church of St Peter de Merton. Here the closure motion was proposed and carried. This formally brought the existence of St Luke's United Church to its end, leaving authority in the hands of the elders to discharge any residual business. Having given thanks to God for 263 years of faithful service to the Gospel, the members shared one last service of Holy Communion and finished with those same words of the hymn by Joseph Hart which Sr Gribble had quoted above.

The former members of St Luke's would now continue their Christian service in their new circumstances. They would carry their memories with them to enhance the congregations they had now joined, and those churches would be strengthened by the witness thus borne – the Christian faith is nothing without the idea of death followed by resurrection. The heritage of the place will never be forgotten by those whose lives were enriched by their encounter with Christ through the work and service of St Luke's, and that will be its lasting legacy.

Appendix: Ministers of St Luke's and Constituent Churches Since 1742

1742	Jacob Rogers
1745	David Hackenwalder
1747	Gottlob Hauptmann
1751	Ernst Ludolf Schlicht
	Anton Seiffert
1755	Frederick William Marshall
	Andrew Parminter
	Charles Gustavus Heldt
1757	+George Traneker
1763	Erasmus Muller
1766	+Philip Henry Molther
1780	John Caldwell
1781	Thomas Yarrell
1791	+Frederick William Foster
1793	+Samuel Traugott Benade
1794	John Hartley
1797	George William Horne
1799	Henry 55th Reuss
1802	John Church
1803	James Gottlieb La Trobe
1806	Samuel Frederick Church
1810	Christian Friedrich Ramftler
1813	Christian Friedrich Harke
1821	Richard Grimes

1824	James Liley
1826	+John Rogers
1840	+Godfrey Andrew Cunow
1841	Nathaniel Rea
1843	John James Montgomery
1844	John Lang
1847	+John England
1860	+James La Trobe
1863	John Lang
1870	+Charles Edward Sutcliffe
1889	+John Herbert Edwards
1894	+Evelyn Renatus Hasse
1906	Samuel Kershaw BA
1911	Robert Bayne Willey BA
1917	+George William Muller MacLeavy MA BD
1918	+Paul Asmussen
1921	Sydney Charles Neath
1922	+Samuel Libbey Connor
1932	Clarence Harvey Shawe DD
1933	Handel Hassall BA
1938	George Alwyn Neath BA
	+John Humphrey Foy BA BD
1944	Wilfred Smith BA BD
1951	Walter Alec Summers BSc
1953	Fred Linyard BA BD
1955	Harry Bintley BSc
1956	George Ronald Lloyd

(Minor variations in spelling in the above names may be encountered)
('+' denotes Bishops of the Unity of Brethren [*Episcopus Fratrum*])

CONGREGATIONAL MINISTERS AT HOWARD

1775   Thomas Smith
1796   Thomas Burkitt
1800   Thomas Smith (second pastorate)
1801   Isaac Anthony
1823   Thomas Binney
1825   Christopher Ralph Muston MA
1832   William Alliott
1868   William Parker Irving BSc
1892   John Thomson
1897   Herbert H Scullard MA DD
1908   Victor Arnold Barradale MA
1926   Clarence George Thompson BA
1930   William Henry Tame
1938   Douglas Andrew Smith
1961   Howard Alan Starr

PRESBYTERIAN MINISTERS

1952   David Davies BA BD
1955   Robert Richards MA
1960   George Harding BA
1970   Harold M Springbett MA

JOINT MINISTERS

1984   Derek A Fitch
1997   David W Tatem BSc
2004   David R Bunney BA

Made in the USA
Middletown, DE
21 January 2020